CONTENTS

T0342874

HOW MUCH DO YOU KNOW ALREADY?

1 What do the following abbreviations stand for in New Zealand?

a) MMP _____   b) MP _____

c) PM _____   d) GST _____

e) QSO _____   f) VIP _____

g) PCNZM _____   h) IRD _____

i) Winz _____   j) VC _____

k) ONZ _____

2 What are the names of the following places?

a) peninsula where New Zealand soldiers fought the Turks in World War 1 _____

b) the country that used to rule New Zealand _____

c) the city which has New Zealand's main government buildings _____

d) the country which has a saint called George _____

3 What are the titles of the following people?

a) the representative of the British Crown in NZ _____

b) the person who keeps order in Parliament _____

c) New Zealand's Head of State _____

d) the head of a city council _____

e) the leader of the political party in government _____

4 What are the following numbers?

a) the MPs normally in Parliament _____   b) the years between each census _____

c) the stars on the New Zealand flag _____   d) the votes a voter has at election time _____

5 Which Pacific Island groups automatically have NZ citizenship?

a) _____   b) _____   c) _____

6 What is needed to finish the names of these Ministries?

a) Civil _____   b) Sport, Fitness and _____

c) Treaty of Waitangi _____   d) Local _____

e) Research, Science and _____   f) Pacific Islands _____

7 At what age can you do the following?

a) vote in a general election _____   b) open a bank account _____

c) get a gun licence _____

8 What is needed to finish the names of the following political parties?

a) The Green Party of _____

b) United _____

c) Christian _____

d) New Zealand _____

e) Progressive _____

9 What special terms are used for the following?

a) written record of parliamentary debates _____

b) a group of MPs studying a proposed law in detail _____

c) a country with a President as Head of State _____

d) a special song belonging to a country _____

e) dismissing Parliament _____

f) agreeing to laws _____

g) changing a law _____

h) MPs voting how they think and not necessarily with their party _____

i) trying to influence an MP _____

j) ancient name for a small room, now Parliament's 'engine room' _____

k) the person in Parliament who wears a wig and gown _____

l) nobody can see how you vote _____

m) place drawn on map for voters to vote in _____

n) place where voters go to vote _____

o) place where government records from 1840 on are kept _____

p) place where MPs meet to debate issues _____

10 What is needed to finish the names of these Kiwi icons?

a) Kiri _____   b) Edmund _____

c) Jean _____   d) No. 8 _____

e) Topp _____   f) Katherine _____

11 In what years did the following happen?

a) New Zealand became a British colony _____

b) New Zealand became a British Dominion _____

c) New Zealand became fully independent _____

d) The Treaty of Waitangi was signed _____

12 What is the English for the following Maori?

a) roto _____   b) kino _____

c) hau _____   d) pai _____

e) iti _____   f) wai _____

12

NEW ZEALAND IS A DEMOCRACY

Government is about the way a country makes its rules and looks after its people.

New Zealand's system of government is called a democracy.

This is where the word 'democracy' comes from:
  Greek **demos** = people
  Greek **kratos** = rule

Democracy is government
  • of the people
  • by the people
  • for the people

	democracy	non-democracy
you can criticise the government (freedom of speech)	✓	✗
government says what newspapers are allowed to print	✗	✓
you can hold and go to public meetings	✓	✗
government says which, if any, religions are allowed	✗	✓
people are allowed to travel where and when they want to	✓	✗
there are free and regular elections for government	✓	✗
everyone has the same rights	✓	✗
there is only one, or not even one, political party	✗	✓
the people elect the government	✓	✗
government gets power by force and violence	✗	✓
government must explain its actions to the people	✓	✗
people's human rights get trampled on	✗	✓
government has to obey the law like everyone else	✓	✗
there is no set of rules for government (a constitution)	✗	✓

Put a tick or a cross in the boxes to show which of the following newspaper headlines could apply to New Zealand.

a) ☐   **General Election set for November**

b) ☐   **Armed take-over puts murderer in control of government**

c) ☐   **Public meeting tonight on government's tax plan**

d) ☐   **Jews not allowed into new golf-club**

e) ☐   **Ten years' hard labour for criticising government**

CONSTITUTION SAYS HOW IT WORKS

A government constitution describes how government is made up and works. New Zealand does not have a written constitution. There is no one written document headed The New Zealand Constitution.

Instead New Zealand's constitution is found in a mix of:
- legal documents such as The Electoral Act (1993) and The New Zealand Bill of Rights Act (1990)
- decisions of the courts which make up what is known as 'common law'
- long-standing practices.

Some BIG constitutional steps for New Zealand:

> You have a constitution. It means how you are made up generally. If your doctor tells you that you have the constitution of an ox, it means you are VERY healthy.

> treaty = agreement

> colony = a country looked after and controlled by a mother country

❶ 1840 Treaty of Waitangi.
New Zealand became a British colony. It did not have its own Parliament. Instead Parliament in Westminster, London, in England, made laws for New Zealand.

❷ 1852 New Zealand got a Parliament.
It could pass laws about how things were to happen inside New Zealand but Britain was still the overall ruler.

> dominion = a country which controls most of its own affairs

❸ 1907 New Zealand became a Dominion.
The New Zealand government controlled most of its domestic policy. But Britain still controlled New Zealand's foreign policy.

> domestic policy = affairs inside a country

> foreign policy = affairs outside a country

❹ 1931 Britain passed the Statute of Westminster.
This let Dominions look after their own foreign affairs. But New Zealand refused to sign it.

> independent = in control of all its own affairs

❺ 1947 New Zealand signed the Statute of Westminster. This made it fully independent.

---

1 Write down the order in which the following constitutional things happened for New Zealand. Write numbers in the boxes to show this.

a NZ Bill of Rights passed ☐	**b** NZ signed Statute of Westminster ☐
c NZ got its own Parliament ☐	**d** Britain passed Statute of Westminster ☐
e NZ became a Dominion ☐	**f** Electoral Act passed ☐ **g** NZ became a British colony ☐

2 Write down the correct term for the following.

a) an agreement between countries or groups _____

b) policy that is about what's happening INSIDE a country _____

c) policy that is about what's happening OUTSIDE a country _____

d) in control of all its own affairs _____

e) a country which controls most of its own affairs _____

f) law made up of court decisions _____

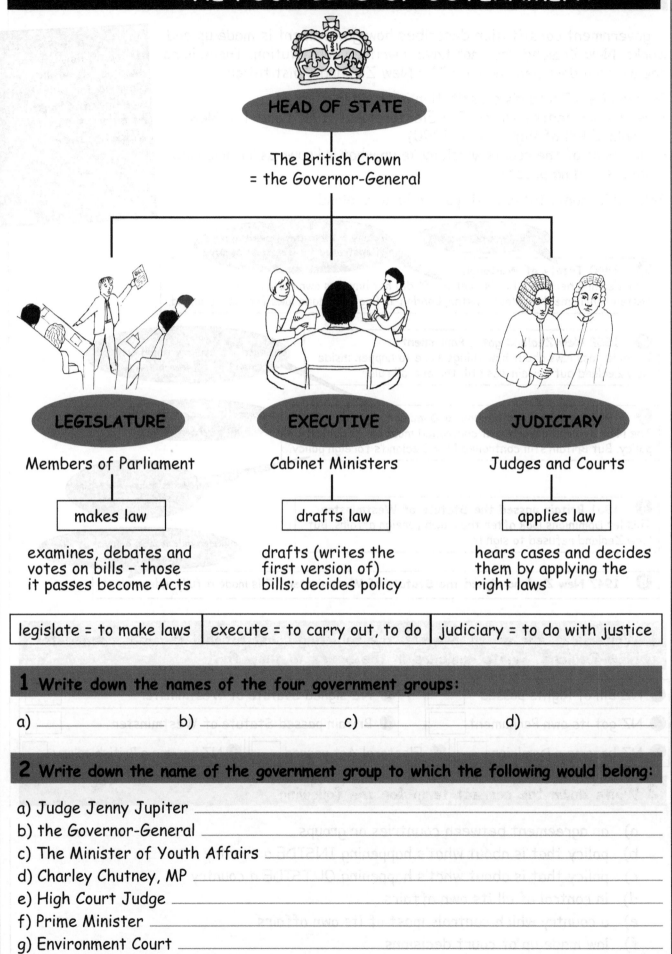

HEAD OF STATE

The British Crown
= the Governor-General

LEGISLATURE

Members of Parliament

makes law

examines, debates and
votes on bills – those
it passes become Acts

EXECUTIVE

Cabinet Ministers

drafts law

drafts (writes the
first version of)
bills; decides policy

JUDICIARY

Judges and Courts

applies law

hears cases and decides
them by applying the
right laws

| legislate = to make laws | execute = to carry out, to do | judiciary = to do with justice |

1 Write down the names of the four government groups:

a) _____ b) _____ c) _____ d) _____

2 Write down the name of the government group to which the following would belong:

a) Judge Jenny Jupiter _____
b) the Governor-General _____
c) The Minister of Youth Affairs _____
d) Charley Chutney, MP _____
e) High Court Judge _____
f) Prime Minister _____
g) Environment Court _____

WHERE GOVERNMENT HANGS OUT

The drawing shows a part of downtown Wellington. Add some colour.

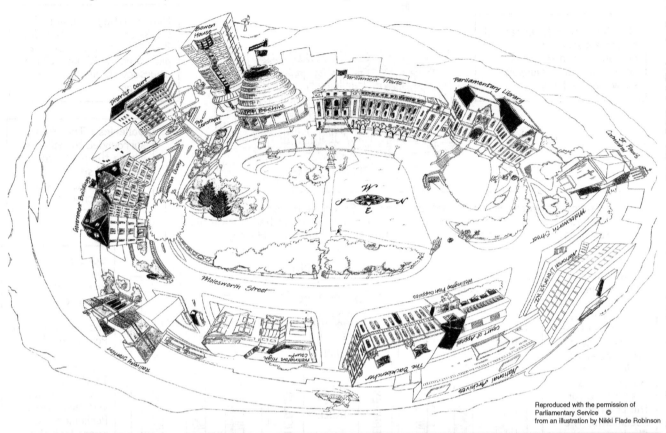

1 Find the following in the drawing and write them down.

a) These two streets are named i) _____ ii) _____

b) This building has ten floors above ground and two floors below ground, has the Prime Minister and staff offices on the 9th floor with Cabinet Ministers on lower floors, and is named after what it looks like _____

c) This has a national reference and research service, and the Alexander Turnbull (history) Library, and is the more modern of the two libraries _____

d) This holds government records from 1840 on, such as the Treaty of Waitangi

_____

e) This building is near the Court of Appeal and its menus feature dishes named after politicians _____

f) A courtroom here has panelling from the Old Bailey in London _____

g) This big brick building serves suburban commuters and inter-city trains _____

h) This is a monument for those killed in war, and has a figure on horseback on the top of it _____

i) Close to the Beehive, this building has a flagpole and wide entrance steps but the planned wing to the south of the steps was never built _____

j) This building, one of the biggest wooden buildings in the world, used to house government departments but now houses the Victoria University Law Faculty

_____

PARLIAMENT HOUSE CONTAINS THE DEBATING CHAMBER

NZ flag = flies from central flagpole above main entrance when House is sitting; lights on flagpole show night sittings.

House sittings = about 30 weeks of the year; Tuesday 2 pm – 6 pm, Wednesday 2 pm – 6 pm, 7.30 pm – 10 pm, Thursday 10 am – 1 pm, 2 pm – 6 pm.

Galleries = The House is surrounded by galleries where the public can come and sit to listen; people who do this are called 'strangers'.

Distance between the two front benches of Government and Opposition = two and a half swordlengths (tradition from old British days when this distance was to stop MPs drawing swords and fighting each other in the House).

Clerk = gives advice on matters of parliamentary procedure to the Speaker and the members, notes down decisions made by the House, and is responsible for the printing of documents. The Clerk wears the traditional dress of wig and gown.

Speaker = the Member who keeps order during debates. Members elect the Speaker when Parliament first meets after a general election. In old British days, if the King was angry with Parliament he might lock the Speaker up in the Tower of London.

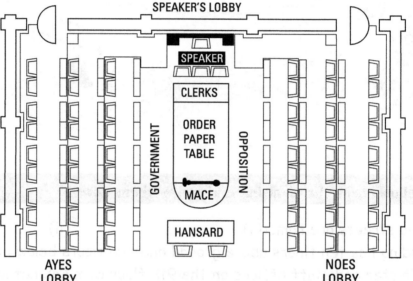

SPEAKER'S LOBBY

SPEAKER

CLERKS

ORDER PAPER TABLE

GOVERNMENT

OPPOSITION

MACE

HANSARD

AYES LOBBY

NOES LOBBY

DEBATING CHAMBER

Order Paper = agenda, daily order of business.

Hansard = written record of Parliamentary debates.

Ayes Lobby = for Members of Parliament voting yes to a bill.

Mace = historic spiked club which stands for authority. It is made of sterling silver gilded with gold. It is about a metre long and weighs more than 20 kg. At the beginning of each day's session, the Serjeant-at-Arms carries the Mace into the House and puts it on the stand.

RADIO

MAIN ENTRANCE LOBBY

Noes Lobby = for Members of Parliament voting no to a bill.

Debating chamber = House of Representatives.

Serjeant-at-Arms = takes the Speaker to the Chair and the Mace to its stand each sitting day, records the attendance of members and keeps order in the public galleries.

Carpet = thick and green.
Seats = leather and green.

1 Colour the drawing as follows.

a) the symbol of authority = yellow
b) the Member who keeps order during debates = purple
c) the written record of Parliamentary debates = blue
d) the agenda = red
e) the doorway for MPs voting yes = black
f) the doorway for MPs voting no = brown
g) the officials who give advice on matters of parliamentary procedure = orange
h) the main entrance doors = pink
i) the seats = green

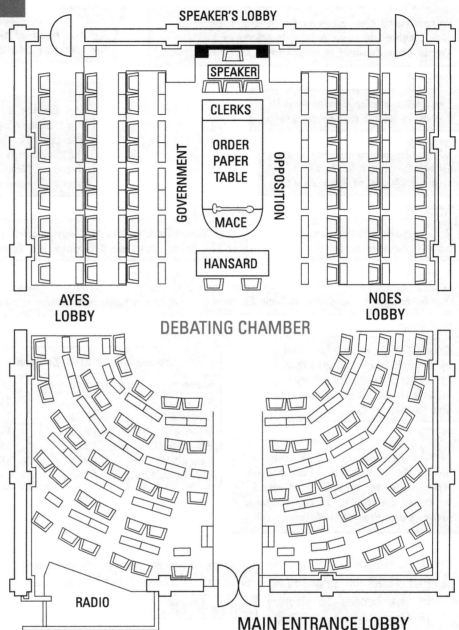

SPEAKER'S LOBBY

SPEAKER

CLERKS

ORDER PAPER TABLE

GOVERNMENT

OPPOSITION

MACE

HANSARD

AYES LOBBY

NOES LOBBY

DEBATING CHAMBER

RADIO

MAIN ENTRANCE LOBBY

2 Now add the following to your drawing.

a) Label four desks 'whips'. (Whips are the managers of the parties. The Green Party use the term Musterer. The Government and Opposition have a Senior and a Junior whip. They have a telephone attached to their desks. They make sure people are where they are supposed to be.)
b) Put an X to show a place where you would sit if you went to watch Parliament. Write beside it the term you would be known as.
c) Show by a labelled line the distance between the two front benches.
d) Above the term Debating Chamber, write the other term for it.
e) Find one 'Lobby' and after it write its meaning in brackets.

FACT 1

Britain ruled New Zealand for a long time after New Zealand became a British colony in 1840. Today New Zealand is independent. It rules itself.

FACT 2

But the head of the British Royal Family is still the Head of State in New Zealand.

FACT 3

The Head of the British Royal Family is known as the Sovereign.

FACT 4

Queen Elizabeth II has the title of Queen of New Zealand.

FACT 5

The British Sovereign lives in Britain, so she can't always be in New Zealand to do things like open Parliament. A representative for the Sovereign is appointed to do these things in New Zealand. That representative is the Governor-General.

FACT 6

A Governor-General can be a female or a male.

FACT 7

The Sovereign appoints the Governor-General on the recommendation of the Prime Minister. Normally it's for a term of five years.

FACT 8

The Sovereign is the Crown in New Zealand.

FACT 9

A crown is an ornamental headdress worn by a king or a queen.

FACT 10

Crown Jewels have been used by English kings and queens for several centuries. They include items such as crowns and swords.

FACT 11

Sovereigns of New Zealand		
Name	Came to throne	Died
Victoria	1837	1901
Edward VII	1901	1910
George V	1910	1936
Edward VIII	1936	1936
George VI	1936	1952
Elizabeth II	1952	

He abdicated – gave up the throne – so he could marry a divorcee.

FACT 12

If New Zealand decided to stop having the British Royal Family as its Head of State, New Zealand would be called a republic. It might have a home-grown President instead.

1 Put ticks or crosses in the boxes to show if the statement fits the country or not.

COUNTRY

Britain	NZ

STATEMENT

a) has a Governor-General

b) used to be ruled by the other country

c) rules itself

d) has the British Sovereign as Head of State

e) is where the British Sovereign lives

2 Find the words that mean the same as the following.

a) ruling yourself _____

b) Crown _____

c) country ruled by another _____

d) a stand-in for another _____

e) a country with a President as Head of State _____

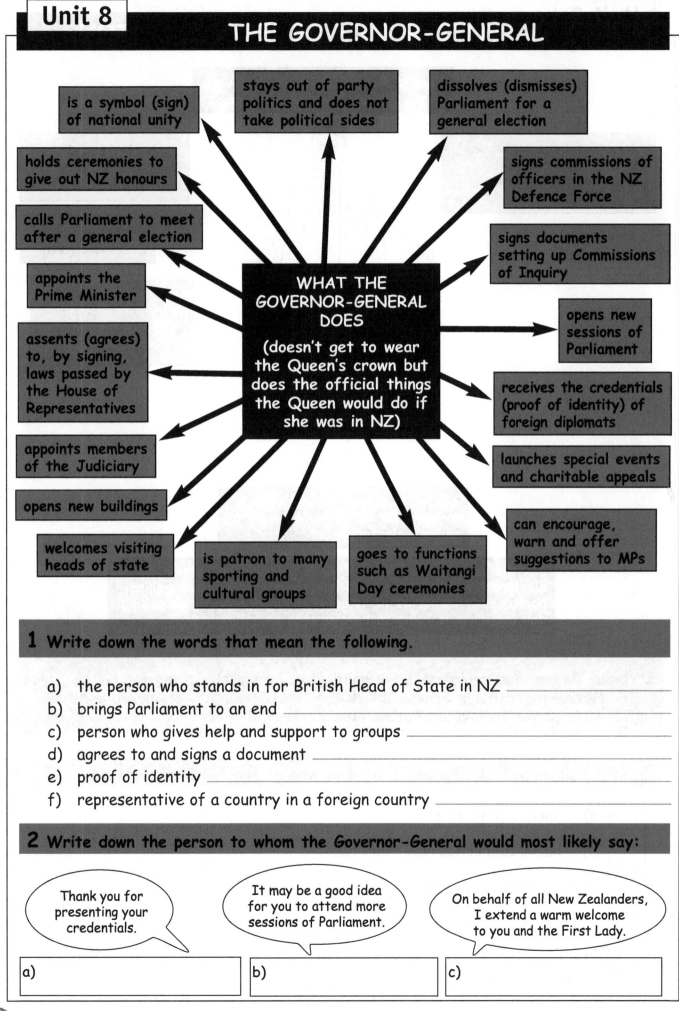

WHAT THE GOVERNOR-GENERAL DOES
(doesn't get to wear the Queen's crown but does the official things the Queen would do if she was in NZ)

- is a symbol (sign) of national unity
- stays out of party politics and does not take political sides
- dissolves (dismisses) Parliament for a general election
- holds ceremonies to give out NZ honours
- signs commissions of officers in the NZ Defence Force
- calls Parliament to meet after a general election
- signs documents setting up Commissions of Inquiry
- appoints the Prime Minister
- opens new sessions of Parliament
- assents (agrees) to, by signing, laws passed by the House of Representatives
- receives the credentials (proof of identity) of foreign diplomats
- appoints members of the Judiciary
- launches special events and charitable appeals
- opens new buildings
- can encourage, warn and offer suggestions to MPs
- welcomes visiting heads of state
- is patron to many sporting and cultural groups
- goes to functions such as Waitangi Day ceremonies

1 Write down the words that mean the following.

a) the person who stands in for British Head of State in NZ _____

b) brings Parliament to an end _____

c) person who gives help and support to groups _____

d) agrees to and signs a document _____

e) proof of identity _____

f) representative of a country in a foreign country _____

2 Write down the person to whom the Governor-General would most likely say:

> Thank you for presenting your credentials.

> It may be a good idea for you to attend more sessions of Parliament.

> On behalf of all New Zealanders, I extend a warm welcome to you and the First Lady.

a)

b)

c)

This is Jay. He is allowed to vote in the general election because

... he has lived continuously for one month in the electorate (place) in which he is enrolled

... he is 18 and over (he had his 18th birthday last month)

... he is a New Zealand citizen

... he has lived continuously in NZ for at least a year at some time

As Jay is Maori, he can choose to enrol for either a Maori or a general electorate

Jay will be a 'special vote' if he is going to be outside his electorate on polling day and has to vote at another polling booth, or if he knows he is going to be in hospital on polling day, or if he is going to be overseas on polling day.

1 Colour Jay in. You could use some political colours such as red for Labour, blue for National, green for Greens, black for New Zealand First, green and blue for ACT, purple for United Future New Zealand.

2 Put a tick or cross in the boxes to show who of the following can vote.

☐ a) Aimee is 17 years old.

☐ b) Shaz is 18 and has never left NZ.

☐ c) Turi is 19 and forgot to register on the electoral roll.

☐ d) Hemi is a 21-year-old New Zealander who has been in Australia for a year.

☐ e) Caleb is a 23-year-old New Zealander who is away on a two-week holiday in Bali when the New Zealand election is held.

This is how Jay votes:

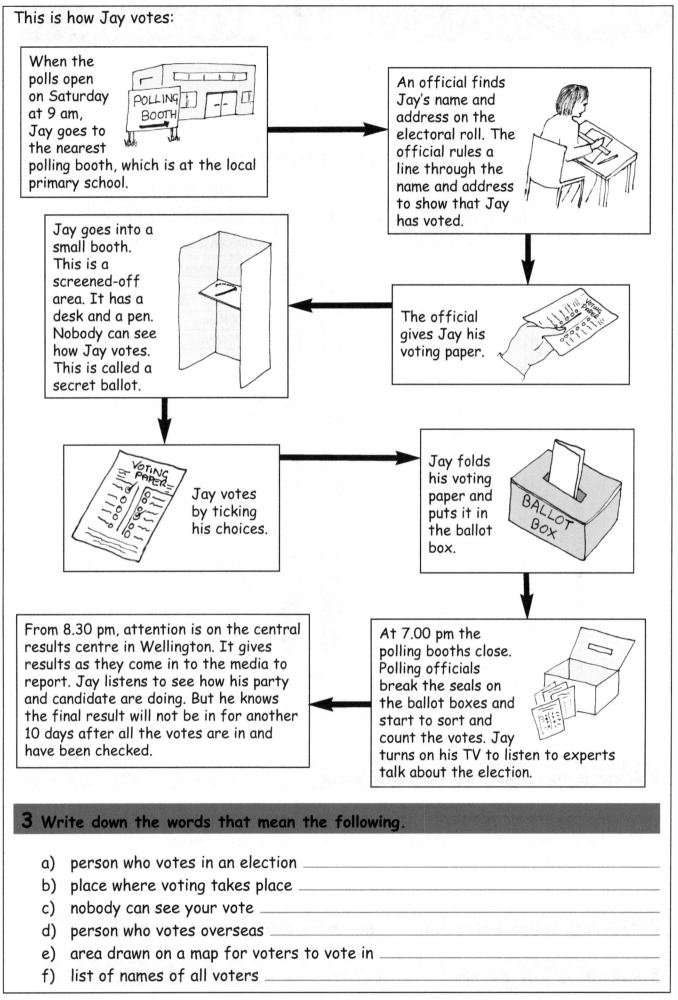

When the polls open on Saturday at 9 am, Jay goes to the nearest polling booth, which is at the local primary school.

POLLING BOOTH

An official finds Jay's name and address on the electoral roll. The official rules a line through the name and address to show that Jay has voted.

Jay goes into a small booth. This is a screened-off area. It has a desk and a pen. Nobody can see how Jay votes. This is called a secret ballot.

The official gives Jay his voting paper.

VOTING PAPER

Jay votes by ticking his choices.

VOTING PAPER

Jay folds his voting paper and puts it in the ballot box.

BALLOT BOX

From 8.30 pm, attention is on the central results centre in Wellington. It gives results as they come in to the media to report. Jay listens to see how his party and candidate are doing. But he knows the final result will not be in for another 10 days after all the votes are in and have been checked.

At 7.00 pm the polling booths close. Polling officials break the seals on the ballot boxes and start to sort and count the votes. Jay turns on his TV to listen to experts talk about the election.

3 Write down the words that mean the following.

a) person who votes in an election _____

b) place where voting takes place _____

c) nobody can see your vote _____

d) person who votes overseas _____

e) area drawn on a map for voters to vote in _____

f) list of names of all voters _____

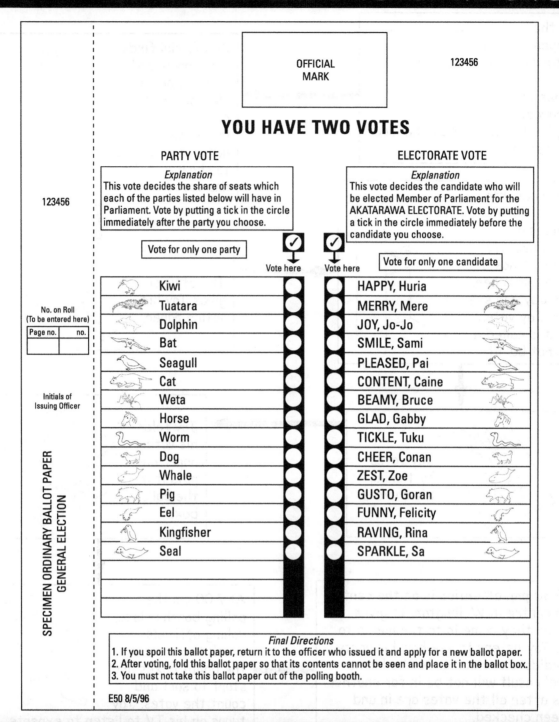

SPECIMEN ORDINARY BALLOT PAPER GENERAL ELECTION

OFFICIAL MARK

123456

YOU HAVE TWO VOTES

123456

PARTY VOTE

Explanation
This vote decides the share of seats which each of the parties listed below will have in Parliament. Vote by putting a tick in the circle immediately after the party you choose.

Vote for only one party

Vote here

ELECTORATE VOTE

Explanation
This vote decides the candidate who will be elected Member of Parliament for the AKATARAWA ELECTORATE. Vote by putting a tick in the circle immediately before the candidate you choose.

Vote here

Vote for only one candidate

No. on Roll (To be entered here)

Page no.	no.

Initials of Issuing Officer

Party	Candidate
Kiwi	HAPPY, Huria
Tuatara	MERRY, Mere
Dolphin	JOY, Jo-Jo
Bat	SMILE, Sami
Seagull	PLEASED, Pai
Cat	CONTENT, Caine
Weta	BEAMY, Bruce
Horse	GLAD, Gabby
Worm	TICKLE, Tuku
Dog	CHEER, Conan
Whale	ZEST, Zoe
Pig	GUSTO, Goran
Eel	FUNNY, Felicity
Kingfisher	RAVING, Rina
Seal	SPARKLE, Sa

Final Directions
1. If you spoil this ballot paper, return it to the officer who issued it and apply for a new ballot paper.
2. After voting, fold this ballot paper so that its contents cannot be seen and place it in the ballot box.
3. You must not take this ballot paper out of the polling booth.

E50 8/5/96

1 Colour in these things on the voting paper.

a) the box that is for an official and not for Jay = red
b) the two boxes that Jay should read before he votes = green
c) the box that tells Jay what to do if he makes a mess of his paper = yellow
d) the boxes that tell Jay how many parties and candidates he can vote for = blue

2 Circle the sentence that tells Jay how many votes in total he has.

3 Make Jay's vote for him.

NEW ZEALAND'S VOTING SYSTEM

- New Zealand's voting system is called MMP (Mixed Member Proportional).
- Parliament will usually have 120 MPs.
- The 120 MPs are elected as either electorate MPs or list MPs;
  for example, 69 Electorate MPs and 51 List MPs.

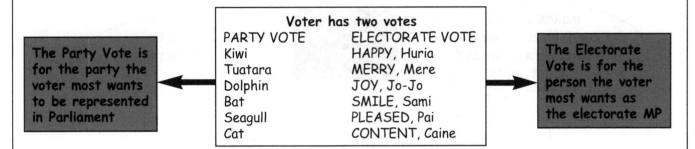

The Party Vote is for the party the voter most wants to be represented in Parliament

Voter has two votes

PARTY VOTE	ELECTORATE VOTE
Kiwi	HAPPY, Huria
Tuatara	MERRY, Mere
Dolphin	JOY, Jo-Jo
Bat	SMILE, Sami
Seagull	PLEASED, Pai
Cat	CONTENT, Caine

The Electorate Vote is for the person the voter most wants as the electorate MP

LIST SEATS are added to any electorate seats a qualifying party has won so it has the right number of seats based on its Party Votes

To have a share of seats in Parliament, a party has to qualify by:
winning at least 1 electorate seat; or
by getting at least 5% of all the Party Votes

ELECTORATE SEATS are filled by MPs elected in each of the 69 electorates:
62 General Electorate MPs and
7 Maori Electorate MPs

Here is a made-up election result.

	Party							TOTAL
	Kiwi	Dolphin	Cat	Rat	Tuatara	Weta	Seagull	
% of all Party votes	41	25	17	6	4	4	3	
total number of seats	53	32	22	8	5	0	0	
number of electorate MPs	35	24	9	0	1	0	0	
therefore number of list MPs	18	8	13	8	4	0	0	

1 Fill in the missing figures in the TOTAL column on the chart.

2 Write down the first letter of the party or parties from the chart to which the following refer.

a) won the most seats _____

b) won the most number of Electorate seats _____

c) won more than 5% of all the Party Votes _____

d) won more than 5% of all the Party Votes but no Electorate Votes _____

e) has more List MPs than Electorate MPs _____

f) has all its MPs as List MPs _____

g) won less than 5% of all the Party Votes _____

h) won less than 5% of all the Party Votes but qualified for a share of seats

_____

i) won less than 5% of all the Party Votes and did not qualify for a share of seats

_____

POLITICAL PARTIES

made of like-minded people

selects people (candidates) to stand in the electorate seats

pools its resources

makes a list of its candidates in the order it wants them elected to list seats

Political party

acts together

has own ideas on what's best for New Zealand

gives voters choices

A party can become the government on its own if it wins more than half the seats in Parliament

Two or more parties that together hold more than half the seats can agree to work together to form a coalition government.

You can register as a political party if you have 500 current financial members.

Examples of past and present political parties:

ACT   Alliance   Christian Heritage Party   Green Party of Aotearoa   Labour Party

Libertarianz Party   United Future Party   NZ National Party   New Zealand First

Aotearoa Legalise Cannabis Party   Natural Law Party   Outdoor RNZ   Progressive Coalition

This was the result of the 2002 General Election.

	Party votes	Votes (%)	Seats in Parliament		
			Electorate	List	Total
Labour	838,219	41.26	45	7	52
National	425,310	20.93	21	6	27
New Zealand First	210,912	10.38	1	12	13
Act	145,078	7.14	0	9	9
Green	142,250	7.00	0	9	9
United Future	135,918	6.69	1	7	8
Progressive Coalition	34,542	1.70	1	1	2
Christian Heritage	27,492	1.35	0	0	0
Outdoor Recreation NZ	25,985	1.28	0	0	0
Alliance	25,888	1.27	0	0	0
Aotearoa Leg. Cannabis	12,987	0.64	0	0	0
Mana Maori Movement	4,980	0.25	0	0	0
OneNZ	1,782	0.09	0	0	0
NMP	274	0.01	0	0	0

Leader of winning party becomes Prime Minister

An MP elected to Parliament is said to have a seat.

Party with second highest number of seats becomes Opposition.

Opposition attacks government policies and tries to show why it should be the government instead.

1
Rule up columns on the graph to show how many seats each party won in the 2002 election. There will be seven columns. Make each one 2 cm wide. Write the name of the parties below the columns. Give your graph a title. Label the axes (horizontal and vertical lines) of the graph.

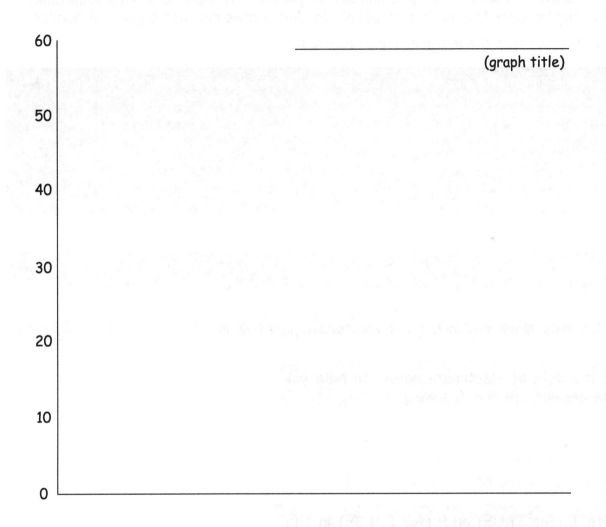

_____
(graph title)

60

50

40

30

20

10

0

2 Look at the results of the MMP election and write words in the following gaps.

a) The total number of seats was _____.

b) The number of political parties that won seats was _____.

c) The leader of the _____ party became the Prime Minister.

d) The _____ Party became the Opposition.

e) The government was formed by the _____ Party.

3 Write down the names of three parties that did not get any seats in the 2002 election but got some votes.

a) _____   b) _____   c) _____

ELECTORAL BOUNDARIES

For a general election, New Zealand gets divided into electorates. These are just lines on a map. The electorate that contains the place where YOU live, is YOUR electorate. The person in that electorate who gets voted into parliament is YOUR MP.

Every electorate has about the same number of people in it. Boundary lines sometimes need changing because the number of people in electorates may get bigger or smaller.

A recent change made these General electorates:

•Aoraki •Auckland Central •Banks Peninsula •Bay of Plenty •Christchurch Central •Christchurch East •Clevedon •Clutha-Southland •Coromandel •Dunedin North •Dunedin South •East Coast •East Coast Bays •Epsom •Hamilton East •Hamilton West •Helensville •Hutt South •Ilam •Invercargill •Kaikoura •Mana •Mangere •Manukau East •Manurewa •Maungakiekie •Mt Albert •Mt Roskill •Napier •Nelson •New Lynn •New Plymouth •North Shore •Northcote •Northland •Ohariu-Belmont •Otago •Otaki •Pakuranga •Palmerston North •Piako •Port Waikato •Rakaia •Rangitikei •Rimutaka •Rodney •Rongotai •Rotorua •Tamaki •Taranaki-King Country •Taupo •Tauranga •Te Atatu •Tukituki •Waimakariri •Wairarapa •Waitakere •Wellington Central •West Coast-Tasman •Whanganui •Whangarei •Wigram

These were the Maori electorates:

•Ikaroa-Rawhiti •Tainui •Tamaki Makaurau •Te Tai Hauauru •Te Tai Tokerau •Te Tai Tonga •Waiariki

1 On the map mark and name the electorate you live in.

2 Use the lists of electorate names to help you write answers to the following:

a) How many of the 120 seats in Parliament were from General electorates _____

b) How many were from Maori electorates _____

3 Write T (for TRUE) or F (for FALSE) in the boxes:

[ ] a) The Tamaki Makaurau electorate, which is the one including the heart of Auckland, and the South Island Maori electorate, would have about the same number of people in them.

[ ] b) Electorates aren't marked by fences or hedges on the ground.

46 electorates

16 electorates

PETITIONS AND POLLS

A petition:

goes to the House of Representatives

must have your name and address on it

is a document that asks the House to take action on an issue

To the House of Representatives

The Petition of _____

(NAME – please print clearly)

_____   _____

(ADDRESS – please print clearly)   *(SIGNATURE)*

and _____ others

Respectfully requests:

That …

can be signed by other people as well as you

can be in English or in Maori

can be hand-written or typed

can be presented by any New Zealand citizen, no matter how old

tells the House what you want it to do (this part is called the prayer)

A poll:

- is a survey to check out public opinion on an issue. Examples are a poll to see if people want an early election; or which political party would win the election if it was held tomorrow
- takes a sample of the population and asks those people the question
- is often carried out for an organisation such as a newspaper or TV channel which presents the results to the public.

An example of a newspaper poll:

ELECTION POLL

Do you think the Government should call for an early election?	**YES**	**NO**	**Don't know**
	30.5%	59.2%	10.3%

Sample size: 650   Margin of error: ± 3.2%

1 Fill out the petition by doing the following.

a) Write in your name, address and signature.
b) Write in your prayer.
c) Find at least five other people who support your petition. Their signatures would appear on a second sheet. Fill in the number of 'others'.

2 Look at the poll example and write answers to it.

a) The question the poll asked was _____

b) The number of people it asked was _____

c) The majority said _____

d) The margin of error was _____

e) The percentage totals for replies add up to _____

Just because you aren't 18 years old doesn't mean you can't have your say in how things work in New Zealand. There are heaps of ways to get those with the power to listen to your great ideas.

Get in touch with your electorate MP. You can ring, fax, e-mail, write a letter, or go to see the MP in person. Let the MP know what issues are important to you. Let the MP know what you, and maybe your friends too, think of a particular issue. MPs aren't mind-readers; they need you to tell them stuff.

You can go to a public meeting being held on a particular issue.

You can join a march or demonstration if you agree with what the people are protesting about.

You can talk about issues with anyone else who wants to talk about them.

You can sign a petition to Parliament about a particular issue. You can even start a petition yourself.

You can write to any other MP by addressing an envelope with the MP's name and adding 'Parliament Buildings, Wellington.' You don't even need a stamp. If you have an opinion or idea, let the MP concerned know about it.

Put a cross or a tick in the boxes to show whether or not someone below the age of 18 is allowed to do the things mentioned.

a) start a petition to Parliament ☐

b) talk about issues ☐

c) join a march or demonstration ☐

d) sign a petition to Parliament ☐

e) ring your electorate MP ☐

f) vote in a general election ☐

g) fax or e-mail your electorate MP ☐

h) write a letter to an MP ☐

i) write a letter to the editor of a newspaper ☐

j) go to a public meeting ☐

k) stand for Parliament ☐

l) go to visit your electorate MP ☐

WHAT MEMBERS OF PARLIAMENT DO

go to sittings of the House of Representatives

take part in debates in the House

serve on committees and become experts on the committee's topic

reply to hundreds, maybe thousands, of letters a year

keep up with what's happening in NZ

be loyal to their political pary

keep up with important world events

get interviewed on TV

give speeches

write articles for the media

meet VIPs (very important people)

hold clinics for their electorates on Saturdays

go to public functions

listen to people who want help with getting their ideas given to Parliament

1 Write down the words that mean the following.

a) a discussion of a public question _____

b) ways by which news is passed on such as radio, TV, newspapers

_____

c) abbreviation for Very Important People _____

d) a small group of MPs appointed to deal with a special topic _____

e) a gathering or get-together _____

2 Put a tick beside the qualities in the following list that would be good for an MP to have and a cross beside the ones it would be good for an MP not to have.

- [ ] a) interest in dealing with people
- [ ] b) dislike of being in the public eye
- [ ] c) liking for sitting on the fence and not giving opinions
- [ ] d) refusal to bad-mouth the party's leader
- [ ] e) dislike of going to House sittings
- [ ] f) interest in giving interviews
- [ ] g) interest in research
- [ ] h) interest in keeping up to date on current affairs
- [ ] i) dislike of the way some people never answer letters
- [ ] j) interest in mixing with the locals

GOVERNMENT MINISTERS

The Prime Minister chooses some Members of Parliament in her or his party to be special Ministers in charge of Ministries. These Ministers are said to have portfolios. (A portfolio is a leather case for carrying documents.)

Ministers usually have more than one portfolio/Ministry. They may have thousands of staff. They may spend millions of dollars a week.

Some examples of Ministries are:

Accident Insurance	Agriculture	Arts, Culture & Heritage	Attorney-General	Revenue	Biosecurity	
Broadcasting	Civil Defence	Courts	Energy	Commerce	Communications	Statistics	Education
Crown Research Institutes	Conservation	Customs	Consumer Affairs	State Services	Corrections	
Fisheries	Defence	Disarmament & Arms Control	Economic Development	Environment	Finance	
Education Review Office	Information Technology	Police	Foreign Affairs & Trade	Forestry		
Health	Housing	Immigration	Industry & Regional Development	Land Information	Justice	
Internal Affairs	Labour	Law Commission	Local Government	Racing	Maori Affairs	Tourism
Pacific Island Affairs	Veterans' Affairs	Youth Affairs	Research, Science & Technology			
Senior Citizens	Sport, Fitness & Leisure	Social Services & Employment	State Owned Enterprises			
Transport	Treasurer	Trade Negotiations	Treaty of Waitangi Negotiations	Women's Affairs		

1 Write in the missing letters to make the names of Ministries.

a) __ OU __ I __ __ __

b) __ __ __ A __ __ __ __ O __ __ __

c) __ IO __ E __ U __ I __ __ __

d) __ __ __ A __ I __ __ I __ __

e) __ O __ __ U __ E __ A __ __ AI __ __

f) __ O __ E __ __ A __ __ AI __ __ __

g) __ A __ I __ I __ I __ __ __ A __ __ A __ __ AI __ __ __

h) I __ __ __ O __ __ A __ IO __ __ E __ __ __ O __ O __ __

i) __ O __ A __ __ O __ E __ __ __ E __ __ __

j) __ I __ I __ __ E __ E __ __ E

2 Write down the names for the following Ministries.

a) The two Ministries that would be most interested in people of certain ages, such as 100-year-olds and 12–25-year-olds _____

b) The two Ministries most closely linked to schools _____

c) The two Ministries that would be most interested in a proposal to bottle water from Milford Sound for export _____

d) The six Ministries most concerned with law _____

e) The two Ministries most closely linked to Maori _____

f) The three Ministries most closely linked with the producing of goods from land and sea _____

CABINET IS THE ENGINE ROOM

Cabinet

- is an ancient word for a small room
- is where the main decisions of Government are made, such as important spending and international treaties and agreements
- usually meets every Monday
- meets in a room on the top floor of the Beehive
- is chaired by the Prime Minister
- has a big workload – often 20 or 30 items on the agenda
- gives all Ministers the chance to have their say
- follows a policy called collective responsibility, which is once a decision is made, all Ministers are expected to support the decision
- not all ministers are in cabinet because cabinet is a small special group of only 20 ministers who sit in the 20 seats around the oval cabinet table and come up with the important government plays.

120 people were chosen by the voting public to be MPs in Parliament	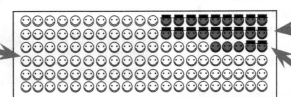	The PM and colleagues chose 23 MPs to be Ministers
		The PM and colleagues chose 20 MPs to be in the Cabinet

1 Check out the drawing which is a way of showing how Government works, and write down the number of the place you would find the following:

NEW ZEALAND GOVERNMENT

a) the Prime Minister ☐

b) the MPs outside Cabinet ☐

c) the Cabinet ☐

2 Write YES or NO in the boxes to answer the following questions.

☐ a) Are all Ministers members of Cabinet?

☐ b) Does collective responsibility mean all Ministers support decisions?

☐ c) Does the voting public choose who will be in Cabinet?

☐ d) Do the weekly Cabinet meetings take place in the Debating Chamber?

☐ e) Is everyone in Cabinet a Minister?

☐ f) Does the PM normally chair the Cabinet meetings?

HOW LAWS GET MADE

Laws are rules for society.

Parliament, representing all New Zealand, makes these rules.

The laws are for all New Zealand, not just one place.

Parliament usually passes between 100 and 200 laws each year.

Sometimes Parliament has to update a law. This is called '**amending**' it.

Sometimes Parliament has to get rid of a law. This is called '**repealing**' it.

This is how a law gets made:

The public can lobby MPs to introduce a bill or not to. **Lobby** means to try to influence.	A **bill** (a proposal for a new law) is introduced to Parliament. This is its **first reading**. MPs don't debate it at this stage. But they read it and think about it.
A **select committee** is made up of 8 or more MPs from Government and Opposition parties. There are 13 committees. They cover all the areas of government such as agriculture and Maori Affairs. transport.	The bill gets its **second reading**. This is the big debate on it. Then it goes to a **select committee**.
The public can make **submissions** on the bill. They do this by writing down their comments and sending them to the select committee.	The select committee studies the bill in detail. They may make changes to it. They send it back to the House.
	The House debates the report of the select committee.
The public can lobby MPs at any time to vote for or against a bill.	The whole House debates the bill.
MPs vote on the bill as it goes through its stages. When they vote according to their conscience rather than automatically voting with their party, it is called a **conscience vote**.	The bill is debated a final time. It gets its **third reading**. It is sent to the Governor-General for **Royal Assent** (signature on the bill).
	The Governor-General assents to the bill. This makes the bill a law. It is now an **Act of Parliament**. Another term for it is a **Statute**. A law or set of laws is also called legislation.

For example:

> In August 1999, Parliament passed the Sale of Liquor Amendment Act. It made changes to the way alcohol could be sold or supplied. Most of the changes came into force on 1 December 1999.
>
> It set the minimum legal drinking age at 18 years.
>
> It said Police could issue infringement (breaking the law) notices for people under 18 who bought alcohol or were found in a licensed premises where they were not allowed.
>
> The infringement fee was $200.

New Zealand's Parliament has been making laws for more than 150 years. That's thousands of laws.

For example, there are laws about subjects starting with just about every letter of the alphabet.

Animals, Boxing and Wrestling, Casinos, Dogs, Explosives (Fireworks Safety), Food, Geothermal Energy, Health, Infants, Juries, Kiwifruit, Litter, Massage Parlours, Nurses, Orchards, Pesticides, Quarries and Tunnels, Roads, Sharemilking, Tuberculosis, Universities, Video Recording, Wine Makers.

1 Write down the correct term for the following descriptions.

a) updating a law _____

b) getting rid of a law _____

c) breaking a law _____

d) trying to influence MPs _____

e) proposal for a new law _____

f) group of MPs who study a bill in detail _____

g) written comments on a bill from the public _____

h) to talk and argue about a bill _____

i) signature of Governor-General on a bill _____

j) bill that has had the Governor-General's signature _____

2 Write the events in the boxes in the order they happen.

EVENTS

3rd reading, select committee, 1st reading, Royal Assent, 2nd reading

GOVERNMENT WITH YOUR MONEY

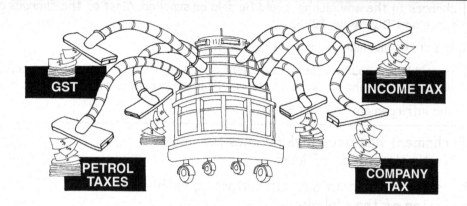

GST

INCOME TAX

PETROL TAXES

COMPANY TAX

Government gets your (taxpayers') money

EXAMPLE
If you earn less than $38,000 you pay 19.5 cents tax for every dollar you earn. $38,000 to $60,000 you pay 33 cents. Over $60,000 you pay 39 cents.

Example: income tax (tax paid by everyone who earns money). The Inland Revenue Department (IRD) collects this each year.

Example: GST (Goods and Services Tax you pay on everything you buy). GST is 12.5% of the price of a good or service.

EXAMPLE
The price of Kim's new jacket was $800 + GST which made the total $900.

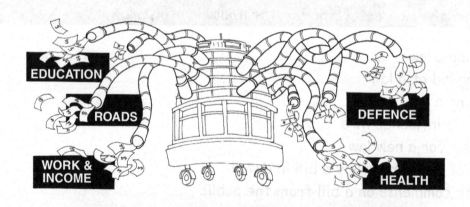

EDUCATION

ROADS

WORK & INCOME

DEFENCE

HEALTH

Government spends your (taxpayers') money

Biggest spend is on Social Welfare. Winz (Work and Income NZ) pay out billions of dollars a year in benefits to hundreds of thousands of people:
• state pension (people over age of 65)
• community wage (people with no job)
• domestic purposes benefit
• invalid benefits
• sickness benefit.

Examples of other big spends are on education, health, law and order, defence.

A person who gets a benefit is a beneficiary.

Each year, the Government writes a Budget. This is a plan for how it will spend money the next year. The Budget covers the 12 months from 1 July to 30 June.

The Minister of Finance reads the Budget out to Parliament on Budget Day.

This is how a recent Budget sorted out how much the big spenders were to get.

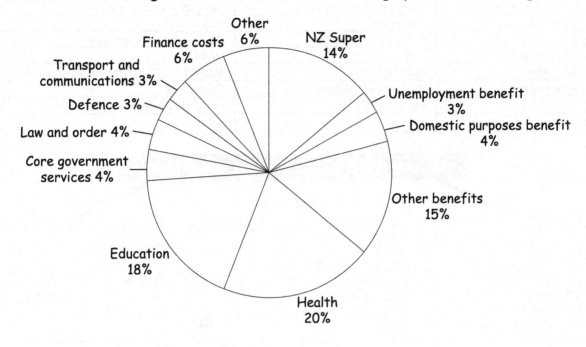

Other 6%
Finance costs 6%
Transport and communications 3%
Defence 3%
Law and order 4%
Core government services 4%
Education 18%
Health 20%
NZ Super 14%
Unemployment benefit 3%
Domestic purposes benefit 4%
Other benefits 15%

---

1 Colour the graph in using this colour code.

red = all the benefits, including super
blue = health
green = education
orange = law and order
grey = finance

yellow = defence
brown = finance costs
pink = transport and communications
purple = core government services

---

2 Write down the words that have the following meanings.

a) money taken out of your earnings by the Government _____

b) tax paid on a good or a service _____

c) department that collects income tax _____

d) Work and Income New Zealand _____

e) payments given by the Government _____

f) people who get those payments from the Government _____

g) a person who is sick or disabled for a long time _____

h) money paid by Government to people without jobs _____

i) money paid by Government to people over 65 _____

j) yearly Government plan for its spending _____

HOW LOCAL GOVERNMENT WORKS

	CENTRAL GOVERNMENT	LOCAL GOVERNMENT
Number in New Zealand	one	a lot
Where they operate from	Wellington	all over New Zealand
Issues they deal with	for all of New Zealand	for just the local area
Name of group	Parliament	Council
Name of building	Parliament Buildings	Council buildings/offices
Name of rules passed	laws	by-laws
Name of leader	Prime Minister	Mayor (City, District); Chairperson (Regional)
Name of members	Members of Parliament	Councillors
Elections	every three years	every three years
Money raised from people	taxes	rates

THE DIFFERENT BITS OF LOCAL GOVERNMENT

12 REGIONAL COUNCILS
- deal with things such as animal and plant pests, oil spills and floods for a whole region
- a region has several territorial authorities in it

☐ TERRITORIAL AUTHORITIES
- deal with things such as water supply just in their local areas
- several territorial authorities make up one region
- some fall within more than one region ⓐ

☐ UNITARY AUTHORITIES
- they are Gisborne, Nelson City, Tasman, Marlborough
- they have the responsibilities of a territorial authority AND a regional council ⓑ

15 CITY COUNCILS
- most people live in urban areas of cities and big towns; for example Wellington City Council has the big urban area of Wellington in it.

59 DISTRICT COUNCILS
- most people live in rural areas of countryside and small towns; for example Western Bay of Plenty District Council has a lot of countryside and small towns such as Katikati in it.

1 Colour in the boxes of the local government chart.

Blue = authorities made up of two different types of councils
Red = councils with more people living in city than in countryside
Green = councils with more people living in countryside than city
Yellow = councils that manage all the natural resources of one large region
Brown = authorities which do jobs of city or district and regional councils
Orange = overall name of all different types of councils

2 Mark the following on the local government chart.

a)   In the box marked in ⓐ write the missing number.
b)   In the box marked in ⓑ write the missing number.

3 Write Local or Central in the boxes to show which government has the following.

a)   by-law ☐   b)   Council ☐
c)   Parliament ☐   d)   Rates ☐
e)   Mayor ☐   f)   Prime Minister ☐

4 This picture shows some of the things that your council looks after. Write down an example of the following in the drawing.

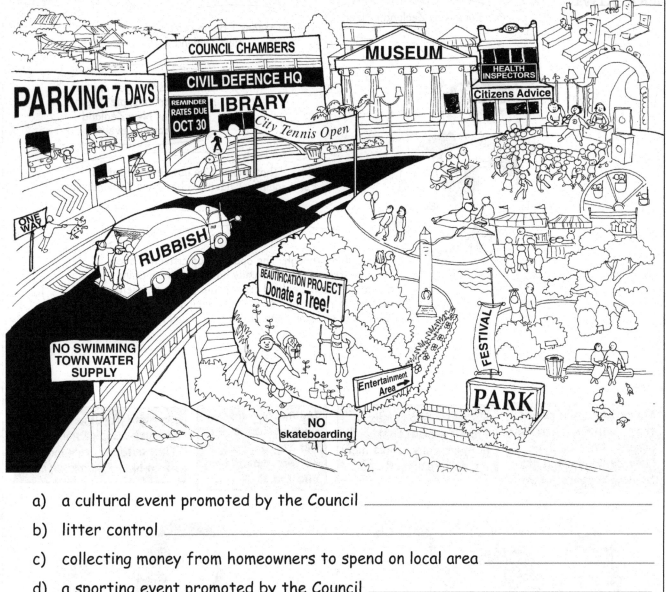

a) a cultural event promoted by the Council _____

b) litter control _____

c) collecting money from homeowners to spend on local area _____

d) a sporting event promoted by the Council _____

e) helping people know the area better _____

f) making the area look beautiful _____

g) carrying out inspections _____

h) giving help during an emergency such as a flood _____

i) waste collection _____

j) looking after transport facilities _____

k) passing by-laws _____

l) providing cultural facilities _____

m) providing cemeteries _____

n) providing drinking water _____

KOOL KIWI

> I'm a New Zealand citizen.

> That means I belong to a country – New Zealand.

> That means I've got certain rights. For example, I can represent New Zealand in a sporting event.

> That means I've got certain duties. For example, I have to obey New Zealand's laws.

> One weird thing though. The opposite of citizen is alien. So my girlfriend, whose family has come from China and not got New Zealand citizenship yet, is an alien. That'll be great, introducing her to the principal at the school ball. 'This is Lin Tan, she's an alien.' Like, what planet is she from?

Kool Kiwi's mates:

My mate Yappie comes from South Africa. His parents have become New Zealand citizens. So now Yappie's a Kiwi.

My mate Tino comes from Tokelau. That automatically makes him a New Zealand citizen.

My mate Ana was born in Russia. But her father's a Kiwi so that makes her one too.

My mate Teremoana comes from the Cook Islands. That automatically makes her a New Zealand citizen.

My mate Sani comes from Niue. He's automatically a New Zealand citizen too.

My younger sister Nik is sometimes my mate. She was born in New Zealand so she's like me – automatically a Kiwi citizen.

My mate Hamish is from Scotland. He's still a citizen of Scotland although he's now got New Zealand citizenship as well. So he's got dual citizenship.

My mate Yasmin comes from India. Her parents want the family to be Kiwis. So they're all applying for New Zealand citizenship.

How much do you know already? page 2
1 a) Mixed Member Proportional,
b) Member of Parliament,
c) Prime Minister,
d) Goods and Services Tax,
e) Queen's Service Order,
f) Very Important Person,
g) Principal Companion of New Zealand Order of Merit,
h) Inland Revenue Department,
i) Work and Income New Zealand,
j) Victoria Cross,
k) Order of New Zealand
2 a) Gallipoli, b) Britain, c) Wellington,
d) England
3 a) Governor-General, b) Speaker,
c) Queen Elizabeth II, d) Mayor,
e) Prime Minister
4 a) 120, b) 5, c) 4, d) 2
5 (any order) a) Tokelau, b) Cook Islands,
c) Niue
6 a) Defence, b) Leisure, c) Negotiations,
d) Government, e) Technology, f) Affairs
7 a) 18, b) 7, c) 16
8 a) Aotearoa, b) Future Party,
c) Heritage Party, d) First, e) Coalition
9 a) Hansard, b) Select Committee, c) Republic,
d) national anthem, e) dissolving, f) assenting,
g) amending, h) conscience vote, i) lobbying,
j) Cabinet, k) clerk, l) secret ballot,
m) electorate, n) polling booth, o) Archives,
p) House of Representatives/Debating Chamber
10 a) Te Kanawa b) Hillary, c) Batten,
d) fencing wire, e) Twins, f) Mansfield
11 a) 1840, b) 1907, c) 1947, d) 1840
12 a) lake, b) bad, c) wind, d) good, e) little,
f) water

New Zealand is a democracy page 4
1 a) ✓, b) ✗, c) ✓, d) ✗, e) ✗

Constitution says how it works page 5
1 a) 6, b) 5, c) 2, d) 4, e) 3, f) 7, g) 1
2 a) treaty, b) domestic, c) foreign,
d) independent, e) Dominion, f) common law

The four bits of Government page 6
1 a) Head of State, b) Legislature,
c) Executive, d) Judiciary

2 a) Judiciary, b) Head of State,
c) Executive and Legislature, d) Legislature
e) Judiciary f) Executive and Legislature
g) Judiciary

Where Government hangs out page 7
1 a) Molesworth Street and Lambton Quay,
b) Beehive, c) National Library, d) Archives,
e) The Backbencher, f) High Court, g) Railway
Station, h) Cenotaph, i) Parliament House,
j) Government Buildings

The House of Representatives page 8
add colour and labels

The British Sovereign page 10
1 a) Britain ✗, NZ ✓, b) Britain ✗, NZ ✓,
c) Britain ✓, NZ ✓, d) Britain ✓, NZ ✓,
e) Britain ✓, NZ ✗
2 a) independent, b) Sovereign, c) colony,
d) representative, e) Republic

The Governor-General page 11
1 a) Governor-General, b) dissolves, c) patron
d) assents e) credentials f) diplomat
2 a) foreign diplomat, b) MP,
c) visiting Head of State

Voting in a general election page 12
2 a) ✗, b) ✓, c) ✗, d) ✓, e) ✓
3 a) voter, b) polling booth, c) secret ballot,
d) special voter, e) electorate f) electoral roll

What a voting paper looks like page 14
2 circle You have 2 Votes

New Zealand's voting system page 15
1 100%, 120, 69, 51
2 a) Kiwi, b) Kiwi c) Kiwi, Dolphin, Cat, Rat,
d) Rat e) Cat f) Rat g) Tuatara, Weta, Seagull,
h) Tuatara i) Weta, Seagull

Political parties page 16
2 a) 120, b) 7 c) Labour, d) National, e) Labour
3 (any order and any of the following)
Christian Heritage, Outdoor Recreation NZ,
Alliance, Aotearoa Legalise Cannabis, Mana
Maori Movement, OneNZ, NMP

Electoral boundaries page 18
2 a) 62, b) 7
3 a) T, b) T

Petitions and polls page 19
a) Do you think the Government should call for an early election? b) 650, c) No, d) + 3.2%, e) 100%

Having your say even if you're not 18 page 20
1 a) ✓, b) ✓, c) ✓, d) ✓, e) ✓, f) ✗, g) ✓, h) ✓, i) ✓, j) ✓, k) ✗, l) ✓

What Members of Parliament do page 21
1 a) debate, b) media, c) VIPs, d) Select Committee, e) function
2 a) ✓, b) ✗, c) ✗, d) ✓, e) ✗, f) ✓, g) ✓, h) ✓, i) ✓, j) ✓

Government Ministers page 22
1 a) Tourism, b) Transport, c) Biosecurity, d) Statistics, e) Consumer Affairs, f) Women's Affairs, g) Pacific Island Affairs, h) Information Technology, i) Local Government, j) Civil Defence
2 a) Senior Citizens, Youth Affairs, b) Education, Education Review Office, c) Environment, Conservation, d) Attorney-General, Corrections, Courts, Justice, Law Commission, Police, e) Maori Affairs, Treaty of Waitangi Negotiations, f) Agriculture, Fisheries, Forestry

Cabinet is the engine room page 23
1 a) B, b) C, c) A
2 a) No, b) Yes, c) No, d) No, e) Yes, f) Yes

How laws get made page 24
1 a) amending, b) repealing, c) infringement, d) lobby, e) bill, f) select committee, g) submissions, h) debate, i) Royal Assent, j) Act, Statute
2 1st reading, 2nd reading, select committee, 3rd reading, Royal Assent

Government with your money page 26
2 a) income tax, b) GST, c) Inland Revenue, d) Winz, e) benefits, f) beneficiaries, g) invalid, h) community wage, i) state pension, j) Budget

How local government works page 28
2 a) 74, b) 4

3 a) Local, b) Central, c) Local, d) Local, e) Local, f) Central
4 a) Festival b) rubbish bins, c) rates notice at Library, d) City Tennis Open, e) Citizens Advice, f) beautification project g) Health Inspectors, h) Civil Defence, i) Rubbish truck, j) roads, Parking, k) No Swimming, No Skateboarding, l) stage for concert, park, m) cemetery, n) town water supply

Being a citizen page 30
1 red = Lin Tan, Yappie, Ana, Yasmin, Hamish; blue = Tino, Teremoana, Sani, Nik
2 a) ii went up, b) i 40, c) iii thousands, d) i) 1975, e) iii Department of Internal Affairs

Ethnic is about belonging page 32
1 a) Iranian/Persian, b) Chilean, c) Italian, d) Afghani, e) Maltese, f) Burmese, g) Lebanese, h) Czech, i) Polish, j) Nepalese, k) Fijian, l) Bangladeshi, m) Filipino, n) Welsh, o) Iraqi, p) Croat, q) Dutch, r) Yemeni, s) Manx, t) Slovak, u) Arab, v) Cornish
2 European = 80.7%, Asian = 64.8%, Pacific Islands = 64.8%, Maori = 62.5%

Census is Kiwis' Big Night In page 34
1 1901, 1971, 2006, 1921, 1926
3 ✓ = 1, 2, 5, 6; ✗ = 3, 4

Knowing your legal rights page 36
1 a) ✓, b) ✗, c) ✓, d) ✗, e) ✓, f) ✓, g) ✗, h) ✗, i) ✗, j) ✗, k) ✗, l) ✗

Human rights page 37
b) employment, access to facilities, c) race, provision of goods and services, d) family status, provision of land, e) colour, provision of goods and services, f) political opinion, employment, g) religious belief, provision of land, h) family status, access to places, i) family status, provision of housing or accomodation, j) age, provision of goods and services, k) disability, provision of goods and services, l) family status, employment, m) religious belief, provision of goods and services, n) disability, provision of goods and services, o) sexual orientation, access to facilities, p) age, access to educational places,

q) ethnic or national origins, provision of housing or accomodation,
r) sex, provision of goods and services

New Zealand's Bill of Rights page 38
a) 13, b) 18, c) 25, d) 16, e) 18, f) 13 and 14, g) 12, h) 11

The rights of children page 39
a) 9, b) 11, c) 4, d) 8, e) 7

Who to go to for help page 40
1 (any order) Commissioner, Disability, Ombudsman, Privacy, Services
2 a) BSA, b) Tenancy Services,
c) Police Complaints Authority,
d) Advertising Standards Complaints Board,
e) Commerce Commission,
f) Race Relations Conciliator,
g) Consumer Affairs,
h) someone you trust or like,
i) Immigration Appeals Authorities,
j) someone you trust or like,
k) Banking Ombudsman,
l) Health and Disability Commissioner, Privacy Commissioner

New Zealand's courts page 42
1 a) Environment, Maori Land, b) Coroners
c) Family, Youth d) District e) Court of Appeal
f) High
2 a) Property damage b) dishonesty c) violence
d) Drugs and antisocial

Ally's jury service page 44
a) ✓, b) ✓, c) ✓, d) ✗, e) ✓, f) ✓, g) ✓, h) ✗, i) ✗, j) ✗, k) ✓, l) ✗, m) ✓, n) ✓

New Zealand icons page 46
1 a) gumboots, b) Beehive, c) Buzzy Bee,
d) Kauri, e) koru, f) hongi, g) kiwi,
h) silver fern
2 (any order) kaimoana, hokey pokey ice-cream, fish and chips, weetbix, Jaffas, Anzac biscuits, pavlova, sheep, kiwifruit
3 (any of the following in any order) Silver Ferns, Edmund Hillary, Peter Blake, Kiri Te Kanawa, Princess Te Puea, Dave Dobbyn, Susan Devoy, Barbara Kendall, Margaret Mahy, All Blacks, John Walker, Katherine Mansfield, Topp Twins, Neil Finn, Jonah Lomu, Peter Jackson, George Nepia, Rachel Hunter, Jean Batten

The New Zealand flag page 47
2 a) Union Jack, b) blue,
c) stars of Southern Cross
3 a) ✗, b) ✓, c) ✗, d) ✓

Why we celebrate Anzac Day page 48
a) ✓, b) ✓, c) ✓, d) ✓, e) ✓, f) ✓, g) ✓, h) ✓

Environmental Care Code page 49
2 a) 390 000 ls, b) 15 000 ls, c) 66 ls,
d) 900 ls

New Zealand honours and awards page 52
1 a) Order of New Zealand, b) Queen's Service Order, c) Victoria Cross, d) New Zealand Cross, e) New Zealand Gallantry Star,
f) Queen's Service Medal
2 a) 2, b) 5, c) 1, d) 6, e) 3, f) 4
3 should be investiture not investigature, investitures take place at Government House in Wellington not Auckland, person should kneel on right knee not left, sword should be flat side on shoulder not head

Maori is an official language page 54
1 a) Pukenui b) Waikino, c) Aorangi,
d) Kaimanawa, e) Rotorua, f) Papakura,
g) Motutapu, h) Tangiwai, i) Rotoiti, j) Te Puke
k) Waiwera l) Pukekura m) Te Puna,
n) Whenuapai, o) Hauraki
2 a) maunga, b) manu, c) awa, d) manga,
e) moana, f) whanga, g) waka, h) whare,
i) pa, j) ika, k) ara, l) ahi
3 a) Statistics New Zealand, b) Youth Affairs,
c) Treaty of Waitangi, d) Inland Revenue

English is an official language page 56
1 a) Wellington, b) Auckland, c) Wellington,
d) Wellington, e) Wellington, f) Wellington
2 a) maiden, b) referendum/plebiscite,
c) Hansard, d) public servant

Why New Zealand is special page 58
1 a) 5, b) Aotearoa, c) she, d) free, e) Pacific
2 C
3 (any order) Wellington, Kapiti Coast, Lower Hutt, Taupo, Waikato
4 (any order) Te Anau, Queenstown, Milford Sound, Twizel, Southern Alps, Canterbury, Takaka, Nelson
5 (any order) Jackson, Middle Earth, Ringwraiths, Hobbits, Tolkein, trilogy

Final challenge page 60

1 democracy
2 constitution
3 1840
4 London, England
5 domestic
6 foreign
7 Governor-General
8 courts
9 library
10 House of Representatives
11 green
12 Hansard
13 Mace
14 Speaker
15 strangers
16 Victoria
17 18
18 electorate
19 Electoral
20 Proportional
21 120
22 Party
23 5
24 coalition
25 seat
26 Opposition
27 petition
28 referendum
29 marriages
30 portfolio
31 Minister
32 Cabinet
33 responsibility
34 Cabinet
35 amending
36 repealing
37 infringement
38 bill
39 Governor-General
40 law
41 Tax
42 12.5
43 Income
44 job
45 budget
46 Wellington
47 bylaw
48 rates
49 Mayor
50 City

51 District
52 citizens
53 ethnic
54 count
55 Rome
56 5
57 fined
58 Premier
59 14
60 18
61 discrimination
62 life
63 assembly
64 ratify
65 Ombudsman
66 Conciliator
67 Affairs
68 appeal
69 punishment
70 Coroners
71 Archives
72 Jackson
73 12
74 God Save the Queen
75 icons
76 Union Jack
77 Scotland
78 blue
79 4
80 red
81 25th
82 Fields
83 Gallipoli
84 land
85 10
86 Wellington
87 June
88 America's Cup
89 red
90 Victoria Cross
91 Cross
92 investiture
93 dubbing
94 Reo
95 English, Maori
96 Development
97 house
98 big
99 maiden speech
100 backbench

Number of applications for New Zealand citizenship granted

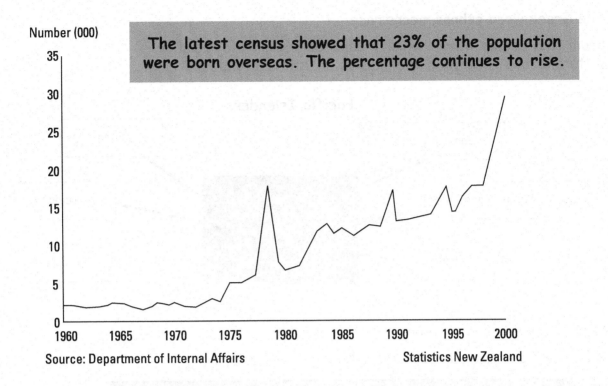

Number (000)

The latest census showed that 23% of the population were born overseas. The percentage continues to rise.

Source: Department of Internal Affairs

Statistics New Zealand

---

1 Colour the boxes red that belong to Kool Kiwi's mates who had or have to apply to become New Zealand citizens. Colour the boxes blue that belong to Kool Kiwi's mates who automatically were New Zealand citizens.

Yappie ☐   Nik ☐   Lin Tan ☐

Yasmin ☐   Tino ☐   Hamish ☐

Ana ☐   Teremoana ☐   Sani ☐

---

2 Circle the best endings to these sentences about the graph.

a) The number of applications i) went down   ii) went up   iii) stayed the same

b) The number of years shown on the graph is   i) 40   ii) 60   iii) 80

c) The numbers down the left side are in   i) tens   ii) hundreds   iii) thousands

d) More applications were granted in 1985 than in   i) 1975   ii) 2000   iii) 1990

e) The government department which collected this data is   i) Department of Internal Affairs   ii) Inland Revenue Department   iii) Citizens Advice Bureau

ETHNIC IS ABOUT BELONGING

The Greek word **ethnos** means race.

From that comes 'ethnic' which means 'belonging to a racial or cultural group'. Everybody belongs to an 'ethnic group'.

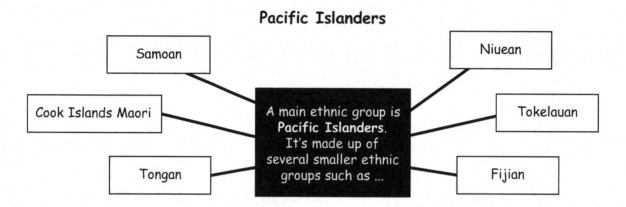

Pacific Islanders

Samoan

Niuean

Cook Islands Maori

A main ethnic group is **Pacific Islanders**. It's made up of several smaller ethnic groups such as ...

Tokelauan

Tongan

Fijian

New Zealand has more than 260 ethnic groups.

We have many familiar-sounding ethnic groups such as:

·Arab ·Argentinian ·Bangladeshi ·Bulgarian ·Croat ·Dalmatian ·Dutch ·Egyptian ·Filipino ·French ·Greek ·Irish ·Hungarian ·Icelander ·Iraqi ·Mexican ·Nigerian ·Palestinian ·Russian ·South African ·Spanish ·Swiss ·Ugandan ·Welsh

Also, we have many unfamiliar-sounding ethnic groups such as:

·Assyrian ·Burgher ·Byelorussian ·Cornish ·Creole ·Gaelic ·Guadalcanalian ·Gujarati ·Inuit/Eskimo ·Kanaka ·Kelper ·Kurd ·Malvinian ·Manx ·Omani ·Punjabi ·Romany/Gypsy ·Rotuman ·Sikh ·Sinhalese ·Tamil ·Yap Islander ·Yemeni

More names of ethnic groups in New Zealand:

Greenlander	Australian Aboriginal	Costa Rican	Fijian	Samoan
New Zealand Maori	Lebanese	Canadian	Vietnamese	Afghani
Slovak	Chilean	German	Chinese	Taiwanese Chinese	Korean
Japanese	Sri Lankan	Iranian/Persian	Brazilian	Indonesian	Czech
Pakistani	American	Jamaican	British	Tibetan	Scottish	Somali
Nepalese	Burmese	Kenyan	Cook Island Maori	Israeli	Maltese
Indian	Tongan	New Zealand European	Polish	Libyan	Italian

1 Write down the names of the ethnic groups that would come from the following places.

a) Iran _____   b) Chile _____

c) Italy _____   d) Afghanistan _____

e) Malta _____   f) Burma _____

g) Lebanon _____   h) Czechoslovakia _____

i) Poland _____   j) Nepal _____

k) Fiji _____   l) Bangladesh _____

m) Philippines _____   n) Wales _____

o) Iraq _____   p) Croatia _____

q) The Netherlands _____   r) South Yemen _____

s) Isle of Man _____   t) Slovakia _____

u) Saudi Arabia _____   v) Cornwall _____

2 Colour the percentages on the graphs in by using blue for children, and colours of your choice for people over 12. The first percentage in each bar graph is for children. Write in the missing percentages.

Proportion of children (0–12 years) in ethnic groups in New Zealand for a recent year

EUROPEAN

19.3%

ASIAN

35.2%

PACIFIC ISLANDS

35.2%

MAORI

37.5%

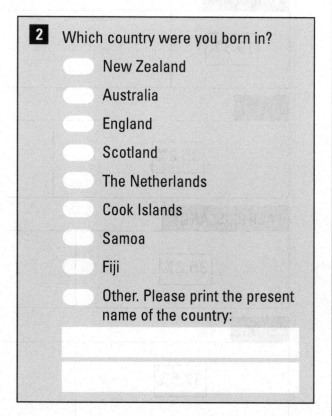

> He aha te mea nui o te ao? He tangata, he tangata, he tangata.
> What is the most important thing in the world? It's people, people, people.

Census:

- is a word from Ancient Rome. The census told rulers how big an army they could raise.

- means an official count of people.

- also gathers information about people such as their age, family, schooling, jobs, where they live.

- is held every five years in New Zealand.

- used to be on a Sunday when most people were at home. Nowadays it's on a Tuesday in March when people are back from holidays and seasonal work.

- asks different questions at different times. For example, people used to have to say how many fowls, ducks, geese and turkeys they owned. The 1901 census asked about Sunday School attendance and the number of servants in houses.

- has forms which have to be filled out for everyone, even newborn babies. You can be fined if you don't fill in a Census form.

- gives information for Statistics NZ to make up tables and graphs about New Zealand.

- keeps records for New Zealand.

- helps plan for the future. For example, if a lot of young families have shifted into an area, the local council would like to know so it can think about building things such as a skate-ramp or swimming pool.

Examples of questions from a recent census.

1 Where do you usually live? Print the full address including, if possible, all of these:
- flat number (if it is a flat)
- street number and name
- suburb or rural locality
- city town or district
- country

2 Which country were you born in?
- New Zealand
- Australia
- England
- Scotland
- The Netherlands
- Cook Islands
- Samoa
- Fiji
- Other. Please print the present name of the country:

3 Mark as many spaces as you need to show which of these is available here in this dwelling.
DON'T count anything that is disconnected or broken.

- a telephone (or a cellphone that is here all or most of the time)
- fax access
- Internet access
- none of these

4 How many motor vehicles (not counting motor bikes or scooters) do the people who live here have available for their use?
DON'T count
- vehicles that belong to visitors
- vehicles that this household borrows occasionally from another household
- vehicles that can be used ONLY for work
- motor bikes, motor scooters

- none
- 1
- 2
- 3 or more

5 Mark as many spaces as you need to answer this question. In which language(s) could you have a conversation about a lot of everyday things?

- English
- Maori
- Samoan
- New Zealand Sign Language
- other language(s) such as GUJARATI, CANTONESE, GREEK.
  Print the language(s)

[grid of boxes]

or
- none (e.g. too young to talk)

6 Mark as many spaces as you need to answer this question. In the last 4 weeks, which of these have you done, **without pay**?

- household work, cooking, repairs, gardening, etc, for my own household
- looking after a child who is a member of my household
- looking after a member of my household who is ill or has a disability
- looking after a child (who does NOT live in my household)
- helping someone who is ill or has a disability (who does NOT live in my household)
- other helping or voluntary work for or through any organisation, group or marae
- attending or studying for 20 hours or more per week at school or any other place
- attending or studying for less than 20 hours per week at school or any other place

or
- none of these

---

1 2001 was a Census year. Circle the years in the list that would also be Census years.

1969   1901   1971   1923   2006
1921   1925   1935   2005   1904   1926

---

2 Fill out the Census questions on this page.

---

3 Four of the Census questions are for everyone in the house to answer. Put a tick beside these four questions. Two questions need only one person in the house to answer. Put a cross beside these.

KNOWING YOUR LEGAL RIGHTS

A right is a fair claim.

Examples of legal rights:

At any age: `any age`
- ★ you can say NO to touching you don't like
- ★ you can't be discriminated against because of your sex, religious beliefs, whether or not you are married, your sexual orientation, age, political opinion, employment, family status
- ★ you can't be treated unfairly or differently because of race, colour, ethnic or national origin
- ★ you can buy Lotto tickets
- ★ you can get a passport
- ★ you must tell the police your name and address if stopped
- ★ you can own land

At age 5:   `5`
- ★ you can be enrolled at a state school

At age 6:   `6`
- ★ you must go to school if you are aged between 6 and 16

At age 7:   `7`
- ★ you can open a bank account

At age 10:   `10`
- ★ you can be charged with murder or manslaughter

At age 14:   `14`
- ★ you stop being a child and become a young person
- ★ you can babysit

At age 15:   `15`
- ★ you can get a car learner licence
- ★ you can sell things to a second-hand dealer

At age 16:   `16`
- ★ you can leave home if you have a place to live and can support yourself
- ★ you can get married with your parents' consent
- ★ you can have a gun licence
- ★ you can get a student's pilot licence
- ★ you can't be taken out of the country against your wishes
- ★ you can leave school and work full time

At age 17:   `17`
- ★ you will be dealt with by adult courts if you are charged with a criminal offence

At age 18:   `18`
- ★ you can vote in political elections
- ★ you can drink alcohol in a hotel

Put a cross in boxes that show people claiming rights they don't have. Put a tick in boxes that show people claiming rights they do have.

	Name	Age	Right claimed
☐ a)	Haile	10	'I'm going to buy a Lotto ticket for my mum.'
☐ b)	Mick	17	'I'm off to have a drink in the pub with my mate.'
☐ c)	Vee	9	'I shouted "No!" when a man touched me and I didn't like it.'
☐ d)	Ra's dad	40	'Ra is 17. He says he doesn't want to go with the family to Nigeria. I say he's going. So he's going.'
☐ e)	Tavua	15	'I'm babysitting my younger brothers tonight while the olds go out.'
☐ f)	Ally	16	'I'm looking to shift into a flat now I've got a job.'
☐ g)	Kat	6	'I want to open my own bank account.'
☐ h)	Dani	11	'I want my own gun licence.'
☐ i)	Mere	15	'I love Stace. My parents don't. But I can so get married without their consent. Watch this space.'
☐ j)	Jay	14	'I'm gonna leave school right now, this minute. Out of my way.'
☐ k)	Don's mum	25	'Don's only 6. He's too precious for me to let him go to school yet.'
☐ l)	Sharlee	13	'Cops stop me downtown and want to know like where I live and stuff, no way will they get told.'

Unit 26
HUMAN RIGHTS

Human rights laws protect people from unfair treatment. They stop discrimination (treating certain people differently to other people).

New Zealand is a leader in human rights. It has a Human Rights Act to protect New Zealanders from unfair treatment and discrimination.

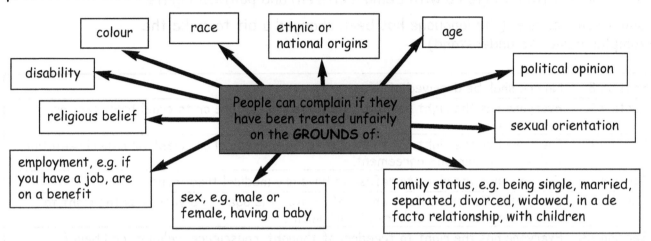

colour	race	ethnic or national origins	age
disability			political opinion
religious belief	People can complain if they have been treated unfairly on the GROUNDS of:		sexual orientation
employment, e.g. if you have a job, are on a benefit	sex, e.g. male or female, having a baby	family status, e.g. being single, married, separated, divorced, widowed, in a de facto relationship, with children	

AREAS it is unlawful to discriminate			
access to places	access to vehicles	access to educational places	access to facilities
provision of goods and services	employment	provision of land	provision of housing or accommodation

(access = getting) (provision = giving)

The people listed here had trouble doing the activities in brackets after their names. Fill in the rest of the table about ways they faced discrimination. The first has been done for you.

SITUATION	GROUNDS	AREA
a) Mo is pregnant (going to school)	sex	access to education
b) Chris is on the dole (joining a golf club)		
c) Philipe is from Nigeria (calling a taxi)		
d) Tai is divorced (buying land)		
e) Dan is black (hiring a plumber)		
f) Kayle is a Communist (joining the Army)		
g) Fran has no religion (buying a cemetery plot)		
h) Olaf has 3 children (booking a motel)		
i) Elle's separated (buying a house)		
j) Dee is 80 (getting a hospital operation)		
k) Lin is a paraplegic (booking a plane ticket)		
l) Benny's cousin is in prison (getting a job)		
m) Hassan is a Muslim (being served in a shop)		
n) Jill is deaf (hiring a lawyer)		
o) Sandi is gay (joining the tennis club)		
p) Tane is 17 years old (going to university)		
q) Lou is Pakeha (renting a flat)		
r) Yasmin is female (buying a car)		

NEW ZEALAND'S BILL OF RIGHTS

Our Bill of Rights sets out the rights that all New Zealanders have.

It's a long document. It's written in legal language so that there is no chance of things being misunderstood.

Part 11 deals with civil (to do with being a citizen) and political rights.

Some examples are: (the language has been changed a bit to make the examples easier to understand)

Section 8:	No one shall be deprived of life.
Section 9:	Everyone has the right not to be subjected to torture or to cruel treatment or punishment.
Section 10:	Everyone has the right not to be subjected to medical or scientific experimentation without that person's agreement.
Section 11:	Everyone has the right to refuse to have any medical treatment.
Section 12:	Every New Zealand citizen who is of or over the age of 18 years has the right to vote in elections of Members of Parliament.
Section 13:	Everyone has the right to freedom of thought, conscience, religion, and belief, including the right to adopt and hold opinions.
Section 14:	Everyone has the right to freedom of expression.
Section 15:	Everyone has the right to show their religion or belief in public or in private.
Section 16:	Everyone has the right of peaceful assembly.
Section 17:	Everyone has the right to freedom of association.
Section 18:	Everyone lawfully in New Zealand has the right to freedom of movement and residence in New Zealand. Every New Zealand citizen has the right to enter and leave New Zealand.
Section 25:	Everyone who is charged with an offence has the right to a fair and public hearing by an unbiased court, and the right to be presumed innocent until proven guilty.

Each drawing refers to a right that all New Zealanders have. In the boxes write the number of the section to which the drawings refer.

a)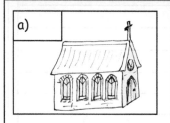

b)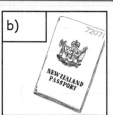

c)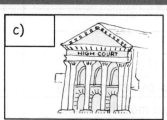

d) Public Notices
Friday 5th November, meeting in Town Hall for ferret lovers to have their say against the proposed ferret law ...

e) Your ticket, Sir, for your flight from Dunedin to Christchurch 11 a.m. today.

f) I have proof that the little green people from Mars are on their way right now to kidnap New Zealanders ...

g)

No way are you going to straighten my nose! I like it crooked.

h)

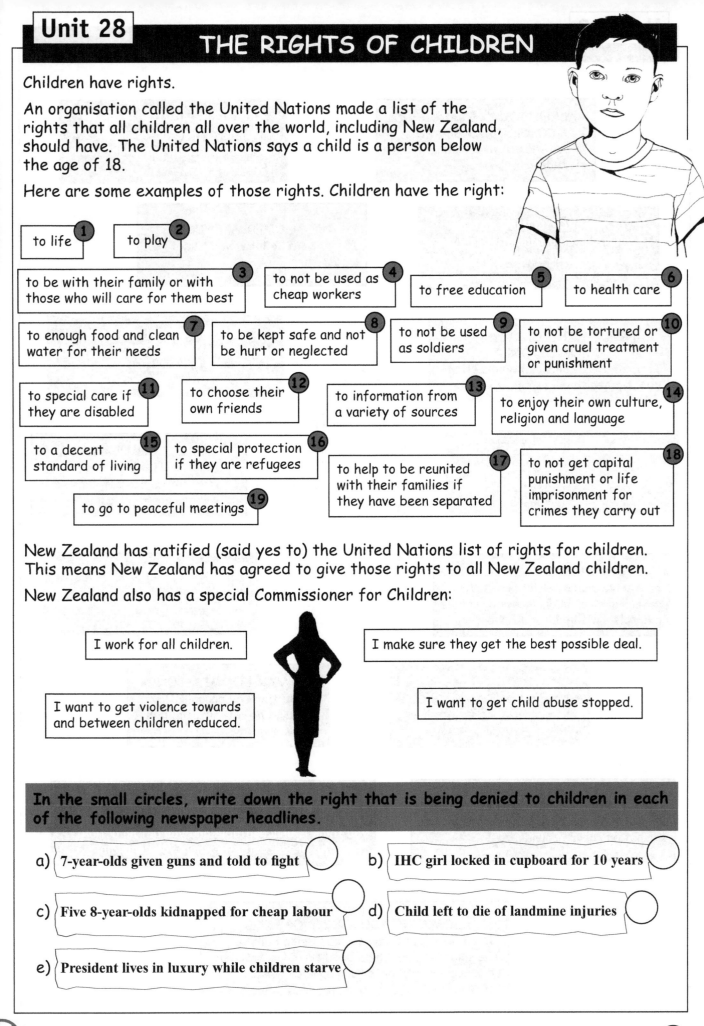

Unit 28

THE RIGHTS OF CHILDREN

Children have rights.

An organisation called the United Nations made a list of the rights that all children all over the world, including New Zealand, should have. The United Nations says a child is a person below the age of 18.

Here are some examples of those rights. Children have the right:

to life 1

to play 2

to be with their family or with those who will care for them best 3

to not be used as cheap workers 4

to free education 5

to health care 6

to enough food and clean water for their needs 7

to be kept safe and not be hurt or neglected 8

to not be used as soldiers 9

to not be tortured or given cruel treatment or punishment 10

to special care if they are disabled 11

to choose their own friends 12

to information from a variety of sources 13

to enjoy their own culture, religion and language 14

to a decent standard of living 15

to special protection if they are refugees 16

to help to be reunited with their families if they have been separated 17

to not get capital punishment or life imprisonment for crimes they carry out 18

to go to peaceful meetings 19

New Zealand has ratified (said yes to) the United Nations list of rights for children. This means New Zealand has agreed to give those rights to all New Zealand children.

New Zealand also has a special Commissioner for Children:

I work for all children.

I make sure they get the best possible deal.

I want to get violence towards and between children reduced.

I want to get child abuse stopped.

In the small circles, write down the right that is being denied to children in each of the following newspaper headlines.

a) 7-year-olds given guns and told to fight ◯

b) IHC girl locked in cupboard for 10 years ◯

c) Five 8-year-olds kidnapped for cheap labour ◯

d) Child left to die of landmine injuries ◯

e) President lives in luxury while children starve ◯

WHO TO GO TO FOR HELP

ADVERTISING STANDARDS COMPLAINTS BOARD
If you see an advertisement that offends you.

CITIZENS ADVICE BUREAU
If you need free, up-to-date information about your rights and responsibilities.

COMMERCE COMMISSION
If you think an organisation is guilty of something like a misleading offer, or wrong labelling.

CONSUMER AFFAIRS
If you want to know your rights as a consumer.

HEALTH AND DISABILITY COMMISSIONER
If you have a complaint or question about a health or disability service.

IMMIGRATION APPEALS AUTHORITIES
If you have been refused residency or ordered to leave New Zealand.

SECURITIES COMMISSION
If you have a problem about investment, insurance or securities (stocks and shares) trading.

POLICE COMPLAINTS AUTHORITY
If you think police officers have acted wrongly in an incident.

OMBUDSMAN
If you have a complaint about the government or public service such as a hospital withholding information.

BANKING OMBUDSMAN
If you have a problem with your bank that the bank has not been able to sort out.

TENANCY SERVICES
If you have a problem with a landlord, tenant or flatmate.

PRIVACY COMMISSIONER
If you think an organisation has used private information in a wrong way.

RACE RELATIONS CONCILIATOR
If you think you have been discriminated against on racial grounds.

BROADCASTING STANDARDS AUTHORITY
If you notice something on television or radio that you think is unacceptable and you get no action from the broadcaster to whom you complain.

SOMEONE YOU TRUST OR LIKE
If you have a problem such as being bullied. The someone could be a good friend, a teacher or school counsellor, or someone at home.

1 Five of the words in the following list have been spelled wrongly. Write out the correct spellings in the box.

APPEALS	AUTHORITY	COMISSIONER	CITIZENS
COMPLAINTS	CONCILIATOR	DISIBILITY	IMMIGRATION
OMBUDDSMAN	PRIVARCY	SERVISES	STANDARDS

a) _____ b) _____ c) _____

d) _____ e) _____

2 Write down which organisation you would go to for help in the following situations.

a) You think a television series contained too much violence _____

_____

b) The 'flatmate from hell' has moved in and won't move out _____

_____

c) You get raided by the police and you believe an officer treats you too roughly

_____

d) An advertisement makes you angry because it pokes fun at your religion

_____

e) The contents of a cereal packet do not match the picture on the cereal box

_____

f) You think you didn't get interviewed for a job because of your skin colour

_____

g) Your new hockey stick snapped during the first game and you wonder what your

rights are as a consumer _____

h) You are being bullied at school _____

i) You are from Pakistan and want to stay in New Zealand but have been told you

have to leave _____

j) You feel unhappy about a lot of personal stuff _____

k) Someone has been using your Visa card and you can't get straight answers from

your bank _____

l) Your doctor has given information about your health to your employer without

asking you _____

A court is a place where law cases are heard. New Zealand has more than 70 courts from Kaitaia in the north to Invercargill in the south.

appeal = to ask for a review of a case by a higher court

COURT OF APPEAL

• based in Wellington
• hears and decides appeals from High Court and appeals after jury trials in District Court

civil = about the private rights of individuals and the court cases to do with these

HIGH COURT

• judges are based in Auckland, Hamilton, Wellington, Christchurch
• judges travel to other centres where there are High Court Offices such as Whangarei, Invercargill
• hears and decides the most serious criminal charges and civil cases

DISTRICT COURT

• many have permanent judges
• judges visit other courts from time to time
• hears and decides criminal cases, civil cases up to $200,000, disputes up to $3,000 (or $5,000 if both parties agree)

1 Write down the names of the following courts.

a) these two are the most concerned with land _____

_____

b) this one is most concerned with unusual death _____

c) these two are most concerned with issues about young people _____

_____

d) this one sits in districts all over the country and has juries _____

e) this one is most concerned with people fighting their sentences _____

f) this one hears the worst criminal and civil cases _____

The death sentence (capital punishment) came into NZ in 1840. It used to be hanging, was done in public, and applied to acts such as arson and robbery with violence. It has been repealed (got rid of).

ENVIRONMENT COURT
- holds sittings throughout NZ
- deals with issues such as land use, water permits, public works, mining, felling beech forests, noise nuisance

CORONERS COURT
- checks out 'suspicious' deaths of people such as violent or unnatural death and suicide

YOUTH COURT
- deals with offences committed by child (under 14) or young person (14–17)

FAMILY COURT
- tries to settle disputes by talking
- deals with 'family' issues such as matrimonial property, child custody, adoption, domestic violence, child support

MAORI LAND COURT
- hears matters to do with Maori land

2 Write down the type of recorded crime the following would come under.

33.7% of offenders were children or young persons

Types of recorded crimes for a recent year
- Violence
- Sexual offences
- Drugs and antisocial
- Dishonesty (e.g. theft, burglary)
- Property damage
- Property abuses (e.g. trespass, littering)
- Administrative (e.g. dog control, immigration)

a) destroying property _____

b) receiving stolen goods _____

c) kidnapping _____

d) vagrancy (having no fixed address) _____

ALLY JONES
55 ARAHO ST
PARADISE

Ally is 21. One day she gets a letter from the court.

Ally's name has been chosen at random for jury service from the Electoral Roll. Her name went on it when she turned 18 and registered as a voter.

ELECTORAL ROLL

JONES, A   55 ARAHO ST

Ally has never had a job outside the home. She could probably get off jury service because she's a solo mum who looks after her two children. But she decides to do it.

Ally and the others talk about whether the accused is guilty or not. They decide the accused is guilty. This is a unanimous decision because they all agree to it.

Ally goes back to court for another two days. The lawyers sum up their cases. Then Ally and the other jurors to into the Jury Room.

The accused is guilty!   The accused is not guilty!

The jury goes back to court. The judge asks Ally about the jury's decision. Ally says the jury find the accused guilty.

The judge says he will pass sentence in a week's time. He thanks the jury for their service. Ally goes home.

Tick or cross the boxes to show whether the statements are true or not.

a) If you are over 18, you can be registered on the Electoral Roll.

b) Had Ally been challenged by a lawyer, she would have been excused jury service.

c) A court is a place where law cases are heard.

d) Not speaking English is no reason to be excused jury service.

e) You can be fined if you haven't been excused from jury service and then don't turn up for it.

f) A foreperson is the spokesperson for the jury.

g) A trial is where a person's guilt or innocence is established.

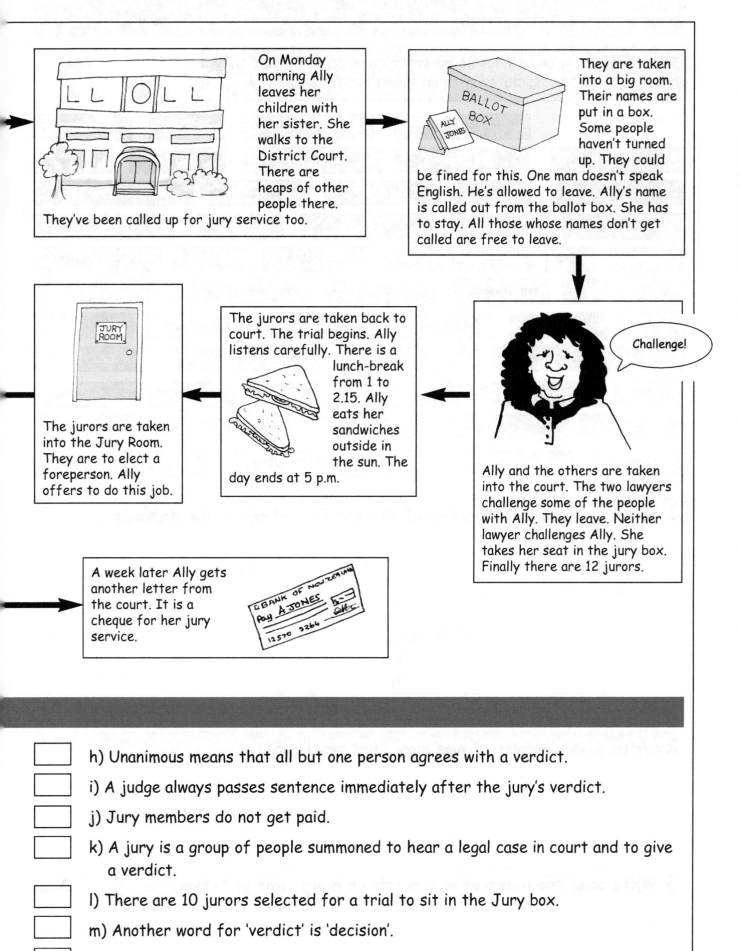

On Monday morning Ally leaves her children with her sister. She walks to the District Court. There are heaps of other people there. They've been called up for jury service too.

They are taken into a big room. Their names are put in a box. Some people haven't turned up. They could be fined for this. One man doesn't speak English. He's allowed to leave. Ally's name is called out from the ballot box. She has to stay. All those whose names don't get called are free to leave.

BALLOT BOX
ALLY JONES

Challenge!

Ally and the others are taken into the court. The two lawyers challenge some of the people with Ally. They leave. Neither lawyer challenges Ally. She takes her seat in the jury box. Finally there are 12 jurors.

The jurors are taken back to court. The trial begins. Ally listens carefully. There is a lunch-break from 1 to 2.15. Ally eats her sandwiches outside in the sun. The day ends at 5 p.m.

JURY ROOM

The jurors are taken into the Jury Room. They are to elect a foreperson. Ally offers to do this job.

A week later Ally gets another letter from the court. It is a cheque for her jury service.

BANK OF NEW ZEALAND
Pay A JONES
12570 3264

h) Unanimous means that all but one person agrees with a verdict.

i) A judge always passes sentence immediately after the jury's verdict.

j) Jury members do not get paid.

k) A jury is a group of people summoned to hear a legal case in court and to give a verdict.

l) There are 10 jurors selected for a trial to sit in the Jury box.

m) Another word for 'verdict' is 'decision'.

n) There are two lawyers on two sides in a court case.

NEW ZEALAND ICONS

Icons are people and things so important in a country that they have come to be associated with or stand for that country.

Examples of icons:

silver fern	Silver Ferns	kiwi	marae
New Zealand flag	Buzzy Bee	Edmund Hillary	Weet-bix	Jaffas
Anzac biscuits	sheep	kiwifruit	jandals	Edmonds cookbook
Peter Blake	pavlova	Princess Te Puea	kauri	Kiri Te Kanawa
Beehive	koru	Mt Egmont/Taranaki	Dave Dobbyn	powhiri	Barbara Kendall
Susan Devoy	pohutukawa	black singlet	Margaret Mahy	Mt Cook/Aorangi
haka	All Blacks	John Walker	Te Papa	No. 8 fencing wire	Jonah Lomu
gumboots	Topp Twins	'God of Nations'	Neil Finn	hokey-pokey ice cream
heitiki	Rachel Hunter	Peter Jackson	hangi	butterflies on house walls
Jean Batten	Pokarekare ana	Beatrice Faumuina	fish and chips wrapped in newspaper
hongi	kaimoana	Katherine Mansfield	*Black Magic* yacht

1 In the boxes write the names of the Kiwi icons shown in the drawings.

a) _____ b) _____ c) _____ d) _____

e) _____ f) _____ g) _____ h) _____

2 Write down examples of nine icons that people eat.

a) _____ b) _____ c) _____

d) _____ e) _____ f) _____

g) _____ h) _____ i) _____

3 Write down the names of nine people or groups who are icons.

a) _____ b) _____ c) _____

d) _____ e) _____ f) _____

g) _____ h) _____ i) _____

THE NEW ZEALAND FLAG

Our flag stands for
- the country of New Zealand
- the government of New Zealand
- the people of New Zealand

Union Jack – flag of the United Kingdom showing the 3 countries of England, Ireland, Scotland.
The Union Jack has the emblem of:
- St George of England – red square cross on a white background
- St Andrew of Scotland – white diagonal X-shaped cross on a blue background
- St Patrick of Ireland – red diagonal X-shaped cross on a white background

royal blue background like the sea and air around the land

Stars of the Southern Cross show the land is in the South Pacific Ocean. Stars are red with white borders.

The New Zealand flag:

has high mana	should be treated with respect	can be used as a cover on a monument at an unveiling	should not be flown when torn or dirty	can be lowered as a sign of respect for the past	should not be lowered just because the weather is bad	can be used on a casket at a funeral	should not be damaged on purpose

1 Colour in the New Zealand flag using the right colours.

2 Write down the colour or symbol on the New Zealand flag that shows the following.

a) New Zealand was once a British colony _____

b) New Zealand is surrounded by water _____

c) New Zealand is in the Pacific _____

3 Put a tick in the boxes beside correct behaviour, and a cross in the boxes beside wrong behaviour.

☐ a) Drew set fire to the flag as a protest against the government.

☐ b) An official covered the statue with a flag before the unveiling.

☐ c) When it started to rain, Bryan raced out and yanked the flag down.

☐ d) The soldiers draped the flag over their dead comrade's casket.

WHY WE CELEBRATE ANZAC DAY

This is a speech that a student gave to his school assembly to mark Anzac Day:

When I think of Anzac Day, the first thing that comes to my mind are the dawn parades on April 25th. I think of the old soldiers in uniform with medals pinned to their chests. I see them standing strongly as planes fly over, the New Zealand flag fluttering high on the flagpole. I see tears well in their eyes as they remember the days of war, remember seeing best friends die beside them, remember wondering whether they themselves would make it home. I think of those men and I thank them. The soldiers who fought in places like Gallipoli were national heroes. They fought side by side to try and stand up for what they felt was true and right. What they felt should be preserved – humanity.

On Anzac Day I think back to the days of primary school. Standing in assembly singing the national anthem. Wondering what the fuss was about. Thinking about cricket or rugby, not thinking about dead bodies or the sea turning red from the blood of soldiers.

But now Anzac Day to me is John McCrae's poem: *In Flanders Fields the poppies blow, between the crosses row on row ... If ye break faith with us who died, We shall not sleep though poppies grow in Flanders Fields.* I used to wonder what that poem meant. What the significance of poppies was. Now I know that wild poppy seeds grow only in churned up earth. It was in places like battlefields that poppies flowered. The Flanders Fields in Belgium, France and Holland were churned up by artillery shells and machine-gun fire pelting into blood-spattered soil. John McCrae wrote this poem after seeing his friend killed. It was his way of trying to deal with his anguish. He wrote it in the back of an ambulance as he looked out the window at the poppy fields filled with rows of white crosses, one of which now belonged to his friend.

On Anzac Day I think of the memorial in the Domain. As I walk by to play tennis with my mates, I look at the list of those who died in service. Men and women who deserved to come home, men and women who gave the ultimate sacrifice for their country. Men and women who didn't live long enough to be able to play much tennis with their mates. It is those men and women whom we celebrate on Anzac Day.

When I think of Anzac Day I think of what the inscription says on the monument at one of the battlefields, Chunuk Bair in Gallipoli. It was written by a Turkish soldier, an enemy of the Anzacs who became a great Turkish leader called Ataturk. He wrote it for the Anzacs and this is what he said: 'You are now lying in the soil of a friendly country. Therefore rest in peace. There is no difference between the Johnnies and the Mehmets [Anzacs and Turks respectively] to us where they lie side by side here in this country of ours. You, the mothers, who sent your sons from far away countries, wipe away your tears. Your sons are now lying in our bosom and are in peace. After having lost their lives on this land, they have become our sons as well.'

I think of Anzac Day as a day of remembrance. A day when we honour those who fought in wars to keep New Zealand and the world free. They fought and risked their lives so we can enjoy the freedom in which we now live.

We must celebrate Anzac Day lest we forget, lest we forget, lest we forget.

Put a tick or a cross in the boxes to show whether the things in the drawings are mentioned in the speech.

ENVIRONMENTAL CARE CODE

New Zealand is lucky to have beautiful wilderness places.

The Environmental Care Code is about helping people take care of these places when they visit.

The 10-point checklist

1	Protect plants and animals
2	Take away rubbish
3	Bury toilet waste
4	Keep streams and lakes clean
5	Take care with fires
6	Camp carefully
7	Keep to the track
8	Consider others
9	Respect our heritage
10	Look before you leave

Caring for the environment means thinking about conservation.
Wasting water, for example, is a no-no.

WHERE YOUR WATER GOES

Action	Water used
cleaning teeth	5 litres
shower	75 litres per 5 minutes
bath (full)	200 litres
toilet (full flush)	11 litres
toilet (half flush)	6 litres
garden hose (on full)	250 litres per 5 minutes
dishwasher (single wash)	40 litres
dripping tap	260,000 litres per year

Toihu te whenua
Leave the land undisturbed

NEW ZEALAND

ENVIRONMENTAL CARE CODE

---

1 Colour in the New Zealand Environmental Care Code symbol. The 'loop' is blue and the 'feet' or 'fingers' are green.

---

2 In the boxes, write how many litres of water were used by the following.

- a) It took Jules $1\frac{1}{2}$ years to get round to fixing the leaking tap.
- b) When Liddy forgot about the garden hose, it ran for 5 hours on full.
- c) Little Peni full-flushed the toilet 6 times before his mother caught him playing.
- d) After their loss, 9 team members had 5-minute showers each, 2 had showers of $2\frac{1}{2}$ minutes each, and 1 had a 10-minute shower.

GETTING A PASSPORT

New Zealand has machine-readable passports. Information is contained in a coded strip which is swiped through a reader at border controls. The details show on a computer screen.

- To get a passport you have to apply by filling out a form.
- It takes about 10 days to process (if there is an emergency, you can get your passport in 3 days).
- You have to pay a fee.
- Children can have their own passports.
- For children under 16 the written consent of 1 parent or guardian is needed.
- A passport is valid (lasts) for 10 years for an adult, 5 years for child under 16.
- All documents sent to the New Zealand Passports Office must be originals. No photocopies are accepted.
- As proof of identity, applicants must provide
  - 2 identical photos of themselves about 50 mm x 40 mm in size, recent, full front view of face, head and shoulders
  - birth certificate.

A passport is an official document which identifies a person wishing to travel overseas

Example of questions asked on the passport application form:

What is your name?
Surname or Family name

Given or First names

Where were you born?
Town/city

Country

What is your Date of Birth?

Day   Month   Year

Are you

◯ Male   ◯ Female

What is your height?

What colour are your eyes?

Do you permanently wear tinted prescription glasses?   ◯ No   ◯ Yes

What is your home address? (please PRINT clearly)
Give street number and name, suburb, town/city, country and postcode if known.

What are your contact telephone numbers?

Home phone number

Work phone number

Mobile phone number

Who can we contact if you have an accident or become ill while overseas?

Contact name

Relationship to you

Address

Examples of declarations made on a passport application form:

- I declare that the statements made in this application are, to the best of my knowledge, true, complete and correct.

- I understand that if I have provided false information this passport can be cancelled and I can, by law, be fined or imprisoned.

Date

Signature of person who is applying for the passport   Day   Month   Year

Your passport application must include a 'witnessed' photograph of you.

You must ask a friend to be a witness that the picture of you is definitely you.

If so, they will need to answer the following question.

Have you written the full name of the applicant, signed your name and dated the back of one photo – all in your own handwriting?

stick a picture
of you here

CERTIFIED TRUE LIKENESS OF

_____

(Full name of Applicant)

_____

(Signature of Witness)

Date _____

Fill out the questions and declarations in this unit.

A Cabinet committee decides who gets New Zealand honours and awards.

There are two regular honours lists:
• at New Year
• on the first Monday in June (when New Zealand observes the Queen's Birthday).

In order of most mana:

People get these honours for outstanding service to the Crown and people of New Zealand. Examples of past and present holders are Sir Edmund Hillary, Margaret Mahy, Dame Kiri Te Kanawa, Sir Murray Halberg.

Members of the Order of New Zealand (ONZ) (limited to 20 living people)

Principal Companions of the New Zealand Order of Merit (PCNZM)

Distinguished Companions of the New Zealand Order of Merit (CNZM)

Companions of the New Zealand Order of Merit (ONZM)

Members of the New Zealand Order of Merit (MNZM)

Companions of the Queen's Service Order (QSO)

Queen's Service Medal (QSM)

Red ochre (kokowai) is powerful and spiritual to Maori. It is used in the ribbons of the Order of New Zealand, the Queen's Service Order and Medal, and the New Zealand Order of Merit. The certificates given with the medals are in English and Maori.

In 1995 Government struck a special medallion (not to be worn) for members of Team New Zealand and others who helped win the America's Cup.

Gallantry = extreme bravery

New Zealand Gallantry Awards

For acts of gallantry by New Zealand Defence Forces and certain other personnel during war and war-like operations, including peacekeeping operations.

1   The Victoria Cross for New Zealand (VC)   most conspicuous gallantry
11   The New Zealand Gallantry Star (NZGS)   outstanding gallantry
111 The New Zealand Gallantry Decoration (NZGD)   exceptional gallantry
1V   The New Zealand Gallantry Medal (NZGM)   gallantry

New Zealand Bravery Awards

for civilians who save or try to save the life of another person and in doing so place their own lives at risk.

1   The New Zealand Cross (NZC)   great bravery
11   The New Zealand Bravery Star (NZB)   outstanding bravery
111 The New Zealand Bravery Decoration (NZBD)   exceptional bravery
1V   The New Zealand Bravery Medal (NZBM)   bravery

There are many other medals people have earned or can earn such as Traffic Service Long Service Medal, Police Long Service and Good Conduct Medal, NZ War Service Medal 1939–45, NZ East Timor Medal, Fire Service Long Service and Good Conduct Medal.

The Governor-General, on behalf of the Queen, holds investiture ceremonies at Government House, Wellington, to present honours. The Governor-General also may give knighthoods. The person to be knighted kneels on the right knee in front of the Governor-General. The Governor-General taps the person on the right and then left shoulders with the flat edge of the blade of a sword and says 'Arise Sir ...' This is known as the 'dubbing'.

1 In the boxes write what the following medal abbreviations stand for.

a) ONZ

b) QSO

c) VC

d) NZC

e) NZGS

f) QSM

2 In 2002 the following people were included in the honours list. In the boxes, write a number from 1 to 6 to show the order of mana (1 = most mana).

a) Peter Jackson CNZM

b) Khalid Sandhu QSO

c) Lynley Dodd PCNZM

d) Loo-Chi Hu QSM

e) Moin Fudda ONZM

f) Gaylene Preston MNZM

3 Mark the four mistakes on this drawing of the dubbing.

QUIET
Investigature
Ceremony
in progress

Government
House
Auckland

MAORI IS AN OFFICIAL LANGUAGE

A special Act of Parliament in 1987 made Maori an official language of New Zealand, alongside English.

It said that anyone in court who wanted to speak Maori could. It was up to the judge to arrange for an interpreter (someone to translate) to be present.

Ko te reo te mauri o te mana Maori
Language is the life-force of mana Maori

He taonga te reo
Language is a treasure

There are many Maori names around Parliament. Examples are:

Te Mana Whanonga Kaipāho: Broadcasting Standards Authority

Te Tari Tatau: Statistics New Zealand

Te Hiranga Tangata: Work and Income NZ

Toitu te Whenua: Land Information

Manatu Kaupapa Waonga: Ministry of Defence

Te Tiriti o Waitangi: Treaty of Waitangi

Te Whare Tohu Tuhituhinga o Aotearoa: National Archives

Aotearoa: New Zealand

Te Tāhuhu o te Mātauranga: Ministry of Education

Te Tari Kooti: Department for Courts

Te Puni Kōkiri: Ministry of Maori Development

Minitatanga Mō Ngā Wāhine: Ministry of Women's Affairs

Te Tari Taiohi: Youth Affairs

Uruwhenua: Passports

Te Tari Taake: Inland Revenue

Ngā Pirihimana o Aotearoa: New Zealand Police

Te Tari Taiwhenua: Department of Internal Affairs

Komihana Tikanga Tangata: Human Rights Commission

Maori is also found in many place names outside of Parliament. These words often form part of Maori place names:

ahi: fire	ao: cloud	ara: path, road	awa: river, gully	hau: wind
ika: fish	iti: little	kai: food, eat	kino: bad	kura: red	manawa: heart
manga: stream	manu: bird	maunga: mountain	moana: sea	motu: island
nui: big, plenty	pa: fortified village	pai: good	papa: flat	puke: hill
puna: spring	raki: north	roto: lake	rua: hole, two	tangi: weep	tapu: sacred
te: the	wai: water	waka: canoe	whanga: bay	whare: house	whenua: land

1 Match the place names in the boxes below with a) to o).

Wainui	Aorangi	Te Puna	Hauraki
Rotoiti	Waikino	Pukenui	Tangiwai
Pukekura	Papakura	Rotorua	Kaimanawa
Te Puke	Whenuapai	Motutapu	

a) big hill _____
b) unpleasant water _____
c) cloud in the sky _____
d) heart-eater _____
e) the second lake _____
f) level land of red soil _____
g) forbidden island _____
h) weeping waters _____
i) little lake _____
j) the hill _____
k) hot water _____
l) red hill _____
m) the spring _____
n) good land _____
o) northern wind _____

2 Label these features in Maori:

a) mountain b) bird c) river d) stream e) sea f) bay g) canoe
h) house i) fortified village j) fish k) path l) fire

3 Write down the English for the following names

a) Te Tari Tatau _____
b) Te Tari Taiohi _____
c) Te Tiriti o Waitangi _____
d) Te Tari Taake _____

Much of the democratic system of government in New Zealand has come from England. The English language is used to describe this system. Some examples:

Maiden speech
- the first speech given in Parliament by a new MP

Backbench
- Members of Parliament who are not Ministers

Task Force
- a temporary grouping of units made to look into a special issue

Hansard
- official printed reports of what's happened in Parliament
- it has the same name in Australia, Canada and Britain
- it's named after the Hansard family who printed the Journals of the House of Commons in England from 1774

Referendum
- a special vote
- when the government has a proposal that it wants the people to say yes or no to
- another term for a special vote is plebiscite

Treasury
- government department which has overall charge of raising, spending and investing Crown finances

Royal Commission
- a person or people appointed by government to enquire into and report on some aspect of public affairs

The Public Service
- part of government
- through their ministers, public servants work for the government
- many departments provide services that touch people in the community every day such as the payment of benefits, provision of passports, and catching imported fruit flies which could damage local industries

BDM – The Births, Deaths and Marriages Registry
- holds records of all births, deaths and marriages registered in NZ
- some date as far back as the 1840s
- in Wellington

The Reserve Bank of New Zealand
- in Wellington
- the central bank of NZ
- only agency in NZ allowed to issue money
- required by law to make sure that money keeps its buying power
- has to make sure prices stay stable
- controls the design and printing of NZ's currency
- issues money to registered banks
- withdraws from circulation currency which is damaged or unusable

Department of Internal Affairs
- provides a wide range of services which touch the lives of all New Zealanders
- examples are organising royal tours, checking out CD-ROMS for pornography, inspecting casinos

National Archives
- looks after government's official records
- makes them accessible to the public
- in Wellington

Premier House
- the official residence of the Prime Minister in Wellington
- classified 'A' by the Historic Places Trust, showing that both house and garden are national treasures and living history
- downstairs used for official functions
- upstairs has a small flat for the Prime Ministerial family

Government House in Auckland
- much smaller than the Wellington Government House
- some of the trees date from the 1870s
- designed as a family home
- the Queen stays at the House whenever she visits Auckland

Government House in Wellington
- across the road from the Basin Reserve
- behind tall iron gates and at the top of a long drive
- the residence of the Governor-General of New Zealand
- two-storied house, with attics, a grand staircase, a ballroom, dozens of other large and small rooms, very long corridors and a flag tower

1 In the boxes write the name of the city in which you would see the following.

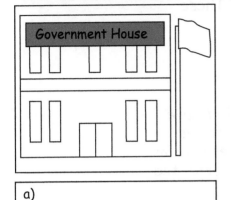

a)

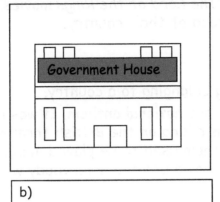

b)

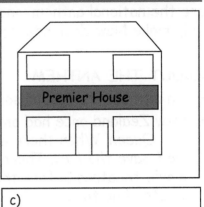

c)

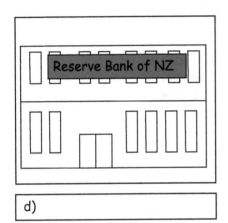

d)

e)

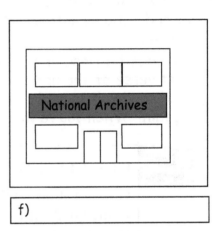

f)

2 In the boxes, write the types of the following.

In this, my first speech to Parliament, I want to talk about this country's attitude to the hunting of whales ...

The government, therefore, has decided to hold a special vote so that you, the people, can let us know what you think of this important issue ...

a) Name of this type of speech

b) Name of this type of vote

Here are all the official records for what went on in Parliament that month ...

I've given 30 years of my life to running round after various Ministers and doing what they told me to do...

c) Name of this type of record

d) Name of this type of worker

WHY NEW ZEALAND IS SPECIAL

Two examples of the different ways in which New Zealand is special are the national anthem, and *The Lord of the Rings* movies. These help make New Zealanders proud of their country.

ABOUT THE ANTHEM

- An anthem is a special song belonging to a country.
- New Zealand once had only one national anthem. It was *God Save the Queen*. When there was a king on the British throne, it was *God Save the King*. This anthem used to be played in places such as movie theatres before the movie started. Everybody was expected to stand up for it.
- In 1977 the Queen gave permission for New Zealand to have a second national anthem. It was *God Defend New Zealand*. It has five verses.
- You can't be fined or put in prison for not knowing at least the first verse of the national anthem. But who knows when you might need to sing it in public. When you're the Silver Ferns or All Black captain? When you've won a gold medal at the Olympic Games?

1st verse	**GOD DEFEND NEW ZEALAND**	**AOTEAROA**
	God of nations at they feet In the bonds of love we meet. Hear our voices, we entreat, God defend our free land. Guard Pacific's triple star From the shafts of strife and war, Make her praises heard afar, God defend New Zealand.	E Ihoa Atua, O ngā Iwi! Matoura, Ata whakarongona: Me aroha roa. Kia hua ko te pai: Kia tau to atawhai: Manaakitia mai Aotearoa.

1 Circle the best answer to these questions about *God Defend New Zealand/Aotearoa*

a) It has three/five verses.

b) The Maori word for New Zealand is Atua/Aotearoa.

c) New Zealand is referred to as she/he.

d) New Zealand is our captive/free land.

e) Pacific/glorious best shows where New Zealand is in the world.

2 Underline the last word on each line of the first verse of the English version. Circle the best description of the rhyming pattern of the underlined words from the following.

a) aaabbccc   b) aabbccdd   c) aaabcccb   d) abcdabcd

ABOUT *THE LORD OF THE RINGS* MOVIES

DATA FILE ON
***THE LORD OF THE RINGS* MOVIES**

Author of book:	J. R. R. Tolkien
Number of movies:	3 (a trilogy)
Names of movies:	*The Fellowship of the Ring, The Two Towers, The Return of the King*
Release dates:	2001, 2002, 2003
Director:	Peter Jackson from New Zealand
Filmed in:	New Zealand
Special effects:	Weta, the special effects company in Wellington
Type of movie:	Fantasy
Story summary:	A group of companions make a very dangerous journey to save Middle Earth
Characters:	Hobbits, elves, humans, wizards, dwarves, Ents, Orcs, Ringwraiths (Dark Riders), Balrogs, trolls
Government:	appointed a Minister for *Lord of the Rings* to make sure fans knew the movies were filmed in New Zealand

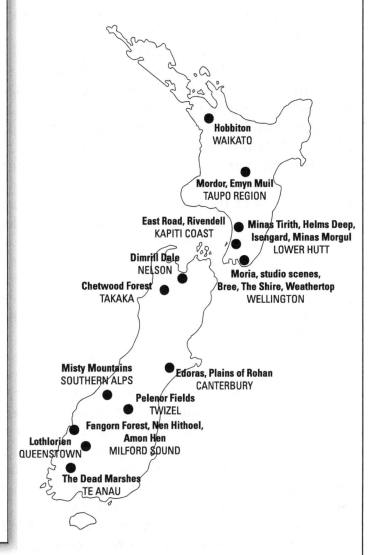

3 Write down 5 filming locations in the North Island for *The Lord of the Rings* movies.

_____ _____ _____

_____ _____

4 Write down 8 filming locations in the South Island for *The Lord of the Rings* movies.

_____ _____ _____ _____

_____ _____ _____ _____

5 Put two pieces from the boxes together to make 6 words important to *The Lord of the Rings* movies.

| JACK | EARTH | WRAITHS | BITS | TOL | OGY | HOB | KIEN | MIDDLE | SON | TRIL | RING |

_____ _____ _____

_____ _____ _____

1   NZ's type of government is called a d_____.
2   How government works is called its c_____.
3   The Treaty of Waitangi was signed in the year 18_____.
4   Westminster is in the city of L_____ in the country of E_____.
5   Government affairs inside a country are its d_____ policy.
6   Government affairs outside a country are its f_____ policy
7   The representative of the British Crown in NZ is the G_____.
8   Judiciary means Judges and c_____.
9   Alexander Turnbull is a famous Wellington l_____.
10   The Debating Chamber is also called the H_____.
11   The colour of the carpet and seats in Parliament is _____.
12   The written records of Parliamentary debates is called H_____.
13   The name of the spiked club in Parliament standing for authority is M_____.
14   The Member of Parliament who keeps order during debates is the S_____.
15   People from the public who sit in Parliament's galleries are known as s_____.
16   The Queen of NZ from 1840 to 1901 was called V_____.
17   The age you are allowed to vote in NZ's general elections is _____.
18   The name of the area drawn on a map for voters to vote in is e_____.
19   The name of the roll that has the names of all voters on it is E_____ Roll.
20   MMP stands for Mixed Member P_____.
21   The normal number of MPs in Parliament is _____.
22   The 2 types of votes are the Electorate Vote and the P_____ Vote.
23   To have a share of seats in Parliament, a party needs _____% of Party Votes.
24   The name of 2 or more parties joined together to govern is c_____.
25   An MP elected to Parliament is said to have a s_____.
26   The party with the second highest number of seats becomes the O_____.
27   A document that asks the House to take action on an issue is a p_____.
28   A vote by the public on a special government issue is called a r_____.
29   BDM stands for Births, Deaths and M_____ Registry.
30   A leather case for carrying documents is called a p_____.
31   A person in charge of a Ministry is called a M_____.
32   The name for the engine room of Parliament is C_____.
33   When all Ministers support a decision, it is called collective r_____.
34   The name of the group which meets on the top floor of the Beehive is c_____.
35   Updating or changing a law is called a_____.
36   Getting rid of a law is called r_____.
37   Breaking a law is called an i_____.
38   A proposal for a new law is called a b_____.
39   The person who signs the assent to make a new law is the G_____.
40   A statute is another term for a l_____.
41   GST stands for Goods and Services T_____.
42   GST is _____% of the good or service.
43   Winz stands for Work and I_____ NZ.
44   A community wage is paid to people with no j_____.
45   The government plan for its yearly spending is called a b_____.
46   Central government is in the city of W_____.
47   Laws passed by local governments are called b_____.
48   Money raised by local governments on property is called r_____.
49   A leader of a city or district council is called a M_____.